LEWIS CARROLL

AS I KNEW HIM

Miss Isa Bowman.

LEWIS CARROLL
AS I KNEW HIM

By

Isa Bowman

WITH A NEW INTRODUCTION BY
MORTON N. COHEN

DOVER PUBLICATIONS, INC.
NEW YORK

This Dover edition, first published in 1972, is an unabridged and unaltered republication of the work originally published by J. M. Dent & Co. in London in 1899 under the title *The Story of Lewis Carroll.* A new Introduction has been written especially for the Dover edition by Morton N. Cohen.

International Standard Book Number: 0-486-20560-6
Library of Congress Catalog Card Number: 78-189345

Manufactured in the United States of America
Dover Publications, Inc.
180 Varick Street
New York, N.Y. 10014

INTRODUCTION

TO THE DOVER EDITION

LEWIS CARROLL first met Isa Bowman in September, 1887. He was fifty-five, a clergyman and Oxford don; she, thirteen, a child actress. She would soon become one of the most important people in his life.

Charles Lutwidge Dodgson (Carroll's real name) first saw Isa Bowman on stage in a minor role in the London production of Henry Savile Clarke's musical dream-play based on *Alice in Wonderland* and *Through the Looking-Glass.* An exceptional child, Isa quickly caught Dodgson's notice, and before long he arranged with her mother to "borrow" her for a day's outing in London on September 27, 1887. It was the first of many such outings and the beginning of a warm and gratifying relationship for both parties. Dodgson took Isa to see an exhibition of paintings in Bond Street, bought her some lunch, and then took her home to her family in east London, where he met her father, her younger brother Charlie, and her three younger sisters, Nellie, Maggie, and Empsie (sometimes Emsie or Emmie). It must have been a memorable day for both Dodgson and the little girl. "I was so pleased with Isa," Dodgson wrote in his diary, "that I got Mrs. Bowman's leave to take her with me, next Saturday, to Eastbourne."

Eastbourne meant the seaside. For a child living and working in London, it must have been an exciting prospect, a real holiday. For Dodgson, Eastbourne was a summer retreat from Oxford. Like most Victorians, he believed the sea air especially healthy, and every summer, as soon as his Oxford duties were over, he would move down to Eastbourne, where he rented a set of rooms in a quiet lodging house near the shore. There he worked on his various books, and enjoyed the town's many delights. Eastbourne was, in fact, one of England's finest sea resorts in late Victorian times. The shore was lined with handsome houses and hotels surrounded by flower gardens, green lawns, and trees; and broad parades ran the length of the magnificent sea front. Attractions like Devonshire Park, with its concerts, fireworks displays, and other entertainments, and the Pier, with a large pavilion— all made Eastbourne the "Empress of Watering Places" and brought to it some of England's best society.

On the appointed Saturday, Isa's mother delivered her to Dodgson for a week's stay with him at the seaside. Before leaving London, Dodgson treated Isa to a matinee performance of a comic opera at the Prince of Wales's Theatre, and later in the day they

made their way down to the sea, arriving at Eastbourne, undoubtedly exhausted, at half past nine. In
the morning, Isa joined Dodgson for church. They
took a long walk together in the afternoon, but, one is
not surprised to learn, Isa was too tired to join her
host for a second church service in the evening.

We don't know what amusement Dodgson devised
for Isa on the Monday—his diary skips that day—
but on Tuesday he took her to a "swimming entertainment"; on Wednesday to a concert and fireworks
in Devonshire Park; and on Thursday, they again
went for a long walk, to Beachy Head and back, about
six miles altogether. On Saturday, they took the
9:55 A.M. train to London, and then spent another
busy day in town, visiting some of Dodgson's friends
and attending a matinee of Buffalo Bill's "Wild West"
show, which Isa must have enjoyed and Dodgson
thought "a very good entertainment." Then, they met
Isa's mother at Charing Cross and parted. Before
leaving Eastbourne for London, Dodgson wrote in
his diary: "Isa's visit has been a success. She seems
stronger and better than when she came. . . . We have
had daily Bible-reading together: and I have taught
her 3 Props of Euclid!"

This first visit to Eastbourne was so successful
that it is hardly surprising that other summer outings
followed. The next occurred a year later, at the end
of August, and again the don and the little actress
enjoyed together the amusements of Eastbourne and
the sea. Dodgson took Isa to an "Illuminated Fete" in

Devonshire Park, sketched her dressed as Little Red
Riding Hood, took her to see *Twelfth Night,* and
arranged for friends to include her in bathing and
sailing parties. And for the first time, they went on
an excursion to Brighton together, where they visited
the Aquarium and the Flower Show. They made
another side trip, this one to Margate to see a production of *Hamlet* in which a friend of theirs was
acting Ophelia. This second Eastbourne visit lasted
a long time—from August 29 to October 3—and when
Dodgson returned Isa to her family, he wrote in his
diary: "Isa has been with me 5 weeks, a very happy
time for both of us." He added: "Isa has been longer
here than all last year's guests put together"; and on
the following day: "Life feels rather lonely without
Isa." Commenting to a friend on the extended visit,
Dodgson is reported to have said, "When people ask
me why I have never married, I tell them I have never
met the young lady whom I could endure for a fort-
night—but Isa and I got on so well together that I
said I should keep her a month, the length of the
honeymoon, and we didn't get tired of each other." [1]

In July of the following year, Dodgson devised a
special surprise for his special guest at Eastbourne.
He tells us about it in his diary: "I had written to
Mrs. Bowman, yesterday, to arrange for bringing
Nellie down for a few days, but kept it a secret from
Isa." He left Isa with one of his sisters, who brought

[1] Stuart Dodgson Collingwood, *The Life and Letters of
Lewis Carroll* (1898), p. 400.

her back to Dodgson at five, after Nellie had arrived. "Her surprise and delight at seeing Nellie was a pretty sight," Dodgson writes.

The days that followed were full of exciting adventures in Eastbourne and Brighton. They went for walks, the two little girls danced for Dodgson's sisters, and Dodgson told them story after story. They went together to concerts, to church, and Dodgson arranged swimming lessons for them. One day he took them out in a boat, and on another they went to a cycle tournament. When the time came for the sisters to go home, Dodgson received a letter from their mother saying that little Empsie had scarlet fever, and so Isa and Nellie remained with Dodgson another three weeks. Ever concerned about his charges' education, he arranged for them to have French lessons. But the fun continued too. They went on two expeditions to Hastings, one by steamer, one by train, more walks, more concerts, and they saw more theatrical performances. On August 27, their visit to Eastbourne came to an end.

On the way back to London, Dodgson and the two girls stopped to call on a friend of his, a lady writer, and she later noted that "the children were bright, healthy, happy and childlike little maidens, quite devoted to their good friend, whom they called 'Uncle' and very interesting it was to see them together. But . . . [Dodgson] did not allow any undue liberties," the reminiscence continues. "He had been describing a particular kind of collapsible tumbler, which you put in your pocket and carried with you for use on a railway journey.

" 'There now,' he [said] . . . , turning to the children, 'I forgot to bring it with me after all.'

" 'Oh Goosie,' broke in Isa, 'you've been talking about that tumbler for days, and now you have forgotten it.'

"He pulled himself up, and looked at her steadily with an air of grave reproof.

"Much abashed, she hastily substituted a very subdued 'Uncle' for the objectionable 'Goosie,' and the matter dropped." [1]

During the academic year, Dodgson was ordinarily occupied at Oxford, and his journeys to London were restricted. But when he went to town, he often saw the Bowmans, and he sometimes took Isa out for a day. Through it all, Isa continued with her stage career. In June, 1888, Dodgson saw her in the Anglo-Danish Exhibition, in London, where she portrayed a little match girl dying in the snow and a Japanese kitchen-maid in two tableaux of Anderson's fairy tales. A little later that summer, while Isa was still performing in the Exhibition, Dodgson took her out on another day's treat, to see various friends and to the Royal Academy to look at paintings. On the following day, he called on Henry Savile Clarke, who had adapted the Alice books so successfully for the stage, to discuss the possibility of reviving the dream-play

[1] *Ibid.*, p. 402.

during the following Christmas season, and Dodgson urged Savile Clarke to consider Isa for the lead.

A few days later, on July 11, 1888, Dodgson came again to London, and again Mrs. Bowman brought Isa to the railway station and left her with him. Together they went to the "Niagara Panorama" that was on in London, then to some friends' for lunch, and to a matinee of *Little Lord Fauntleroy*. And after that, Dodgson and Isa set off for Oxford, where Isa spent the next five days as his guest. She stayed with a lady friend of his, and he came to fetch her early every morning, usually by 8:30, and their days were full of activities. He showed her all the important Oxford sights and landmarks and called with her on friends to have tea. There was so much to see and do that one day, according to Dodgson's diary, even though their day had begun at 8:30, it was nearly ten in the evening before he returned Isa to her lodgings. It was on this visit that Dodgson composed the "Diary for Isa" (see pp. 40–55 below), one of the most charming bits of nonsense to come from his pen.

On December 26, 1888, the revival of *Alice in Wonderland* opened at the Globe Theatre. Not only did Isa play Alice, but two of her sisters and her brother also had parts in the play. Dodgson did not see the revival until January 3, when he next came up to London. Before going to the theater, however, he called on the Bowmans, and Mrs. Bowman, Isa, and Nellie joined him for a visit to the National

Gallery and for lunch. "Isa makes a delightful Alice,"
he wrote in his diary after seeing the production,
"and Empsie is wonderfully good as Dormouse and
as Ghost of Second Oyster, when she sings a verse,
and dances the Sailor's Hornpipe. . . . Nellie sat with
us in the dress-circle. Isa . . . came to entrance
afterwards to wish us good-bye."

Dodgson was not alone in his praise. One newspaper critic confessed that he "could have hugged
without hurting the dear sleepy little dormouse so
cleverly represented by Miss Emmie Bowman, who
with her tiny voice made everybody understand clearly
all that she had to say. Miss Isa Bowman," he
continued, "made a pretty, engaging, and highly
intelligent exponent of the part of Alice, and, although
her singing voice was hardly strong enough to do
justice to the songs, her dancing and her acting
generally secured warm admiration." [1] Another re-
viewer also enjoyed the play. "We have a charming
spirituelle Alice in Miss Isa Bowman, who sings
sweetly and dances gracefully, a quaint Dormouse in
tiny Miss Emmie Bowman, and a funny little White
Rabbit in Master Charles Bowman." [2]

Dodgson tells in even more detail, in a letter to
another little girl, what he thought of the revival:
"It was ever so much better than in 1886: and I think
my little friend, Isa Bowman, was a more refined and
intelligent Alice even than Phoebe Carol, though *she*

[1] *Era,* December 29, 1888, p. 18.
[2] *Theatre,* XIII (February 1, 1889), 116.

was a very good one. Little Empsie Bowman . . . was
delicious as the Dormouse, and as the dancing oyster-
ghost."

At the end of March, Dodgson was again in London
and this time went to see Isa and Nellie act in
Shakespeare's *Richard III:* "Isa . . . [was] good as
the little Duke of York: and Nellie as Clarence's son,
was sweetness itself. I went round, according to
promise, after the 3rd act, to see the children." As
good as Isa was, Dodgson thought she could improve
her delivery, and he wrote her the long letter on pp.
82–86 below, to help her with some of the lines.

That autumn the three elder Bowman girls left with
their mother on a tour of the United States, for the
sisters were to act with Richard Mansfield in *Richard
III* and other plays. Dodgson, of course, wrote to
the Bowmans while they were on tour, he sent Isa
lessons to do, and he received letters in return and
copies of reviews from the American papers.

On December 12, while the Bowmans were acting
in New York, Dodgson went to his publisher in
London to write inscriptions in copies of his new
book, *Sylvie and Bruno.* The book is dedicated to Isa,
and the dedication takes the form of a double acrostic,
the one that Isa includes on pp. 120–121 below. But
it was not until the following May, after the Bowmans
returned to England, that Dodgson sent Isa her special
copy of the book. Ironically enough, Isa did not
realize when she received the book that her name had
been mysteriously worked into the dedication verses.

"She was so long, without finding it out, that I've had to give her a hint," Dodgson wrote to a mutual friend, "and I don't yet know whether she has found out that it comes in in two different ways."

All the while, Isa was growing up. On July 4, 1890, Dodgson notes in his diary: "Day fixed for Isa's Confirmation. God bless her!" But Isa at sixteen still valued the friendship, and the London outings continued—and so did the Eastbourne visits. In September, Isa spent a week with Dodgson at Eastbourne. And it must have been about this time that he asked his friend, the actress Ellen Terry, to recommend an elocution teacher for Isa. Miss Terry herself undertook to give the little actress lessons. "It never crossed my thoughts that you would give her any lessons *yourself!*" Dodgson wrote to Miss Terry in gratitude.

In September, 1891, Isa went to Eastbourne again, for her fifth visit there with Dodgson, and stayed almost three weeks. Soon after this visit, Dodgson arranged for Isa to have singing lessons. In May of the following year, when he visited the Bowmans, and Isa entertained them by singing, he noted in his diary that "her voice has gained strength under Mademoiselle de Bunsen."

In June, 1892, Isa accompanied Dodgson to Oxford for another visit and stayed five days. But there was no visit to Eastbourne that summer, nor in any summer thereafter. Perhaps Victorian propriety no longer permitted the young actress, now eighteen, to be the house guest of a bachelor. Perhaps Isa's interests were developing in other directions. Still, they remained in touch, and Dodgson's affection did not wane. On August 27, 1893, his diary records that he ordered a watch, which, if it turned out to be good, he planned to send to Isa. And he wrote the delightful letter on pp. 62–66 below soon after.

All the same, visits became less frequent as the Bowman girls got more and more involved in their stage careers, and a whole year passed from April, 1894, to April, 1895, without a mention of a meeting anywhere.

Then, on May 28, 1895, Isa paid Dodgson an unexpected visit. She had the leading female part in a musical comedy playing in Oxford, and she came to see her old friend. On this occasion, she apparently told Dodgson of her engagement to be married. On the next day, she brought her young man to see him, and he records in his diary that he gave them dinner at 3:30 and had a number of friends in to meet them, including the famous painter William Holman Hunt, "that Isa might have the memory of having met him."

Charles Dodgson never saw Isa Bowman again. The last mention of Isa in Dodgson's papers comes in a letter to a mutual friend dated November 19, 1896: "It's a long time since I've heard from Isa: and I don't even know whether the report is true, that I heard some months ago, that she is married." Dodgson died fourteen months later, on January 14, 1898.

Although Isa Bowman seems to have neglected her "Uncle Charles" during the last few years of his life, she certainly balanced the scales by honoring his memory with this charming memoir, written the year after his death. It first appeared in England as a Christmas book in 1899 and in the United States the following year. The original title page is curious in crediting the book to "the Real Alice in Wonderland, Miss Isa Bowman." Perhaps Miss Bowman's publisher insisted on a link with *Alice in Wonderland* as early in the book as possible. Although Isa Bowman was, in no way, the real Alice, she was one of Dodgson's *"chiefest* of child-friends," distinction enough for anyone. It is high time that her delightful reminiscence became available once more to all wanderers through Wonderland.

MORTON N. COHEN

New York, 1972

CONTENTS

xvii

LIST OF ILLUSTRATIONS

LEWIS CARROLL

AS I KNEW HIM

LEWIS CARROLL

It seems to me a very difficult task to sit down at a desk and write "reminiscences" of a friend who has gone from us all.

It is not easy to make an effort and to remember all the little personalia of some one one has loved very much, and by whom one has been loved. And yet it is in a measure one's duty to tell the world something of the inner life of a famous man; and Lewis Carroll was so wonderful a personality, and so good a man, that if my pen dragged ever so slowly, I feel that I can at least tell something of his life which is worthy the telling.

Writing with the sense of his loss still heavy upon me, I must of necessity colour my account with sadness. I am not in the ordinary sense a biographer. I cannot set down a critical estimate, a cold, dispassionate summing-up of a man I loved; but I can write of a few things that happened when I was a little girl, and when he used to say to me that I was "*his* little girl."

The gracious presence of Lewis Carroll is with us no longer. Never again will his hand hold mine, and I shall never hear his voice more in this world. For ever while I live that kindly influence will be gone from my life, and the "Friend of little Children" has left us.

And yet in the full sorrow of it all I find some note of comfort. He was so good and sweet, so tender and kind, so certain that there was another and more beautiful life waiting for us, that I know, even as if I heard him telling it to me, that some time I shall meet him once more.

In all the noise and excitement of London, amid all the distractions of a stage life, I know this, and his presence is often very near to me, and the kindly voice is often at my ear as it was in the old days.

To have even known such a man as he was is an inestimable boon. To have been with him for so long as a child, to have known so intimately the man who above all others has understood childhood, is indeed a memory on which to look back with thanksgiving and with tears.

Now that I am no longer "his little girl," now that he is dead and my life is so different from the quiet life he led, I can yet feel the old charm, I can still be glad that he has kissed me and that we were friends. Little girl and grave professor! it is a strange combination. Grave professor and little girl! how curious it sounds! yet strange and curious as it may seem, it was so, and the little girl, now a little girl no longer, offers this last loving tribute to the friend and teacher she loved so well. For ever that voice is still; be it mine to revive some ancient memories of it.

First, however, as I have essayed to be some sort of a biographer, I feel that before I let my pen run easily over the tale of my intimate knowledge of Lewis Carroll I must put down very shortly some facts about his life.

The Rev. Charles Lutwidge Dodgson died when he was sixty-six years old, and when his famous book, "Alice in Wonderland," had been published for thirty-three years. He was born at Daresbury, in Cheshire, and his father was the Rev. Charles Dodgson. The first years of his life were spent at Daresbury, but afterwards the family went to live at a place called Croft, in Yorkshire. He went first to a private school in Yorkshire and then to Rugby, where he spent years that he always remembered as very happy ones. In 1850 he went to Christ Church, Oxford, and from that time till the year of his death he was inseparably connected with "The House," as Christ Church college is generally called, from its Latin name "Ædes Christi," which means, literally translated, the House of Christ.

There he won great distinction as a scholar of mathematics, and wrote many abstruse and learned books, very different from " Alice in Wonderland." There is a tale that when the Queen had read " Alice in Wonderland " she was so pleased that she asked for more books by the same author. Lewis Carroll was written to, and back, with the name of Charles Dodgson on the title-page, came a number of the very dryest books about Algebra and Euclid that you can imagine.

Still, even in mathematics his whimsical fancy was sometimes suffered to peep out, and little girls who learnt the rudiments of calculation at his knee found the path they had imagined so thorny set about with roses by reason of the delightful fun with which he would turn a task into a joy. But when the fun was over the little girl would find that she had learnt the lesson (all unknowingly) just the same. Happy little girls who had such a master. The old rhyme—

" Multiplication is vexation,
Division is as bad,
The rule of three doth puzzle me,
And Practice drives me mad "—

would never need to have been written had all arithmetic lessons been like the arithmetic lessons given by Charles Dodgson to his little friends.

As a lecturer to his grown-up pupils he was also surprisingly lucid, and under his deft treatment the knottiest of problems were quickly smoothed out and made easy for his hearers to comprehend. "I always hated mathematics at school," an ex-pupil of his told me a little while ago, "but when I went up to Oxford I learnt from Mr. Dodgson to look upon my mathematics as the most delightful of all my studies. His lectures were never dry."

For twenty-six years he lectured at Oxford, finally giving up his post in 1881. From that time to the time of his death he remained in his college, taking no actual part in the tuition, but still enjoying the Fellowship that he had won in 1861.

This is an official account, a brief sketch of an intensely interesting life. It tells little save that Lewis Carroll was a clever mathematician

LEWIS CARROLL'S ROOM IN OXFORD IN WHICH "ALICE IN WONDERLAND" WAS WRITTEN

and a sympathetic teacher; it shall be my
work to present him as he was from a more
human point of view.

Lewis Carroll was a man of medium height.
When I knew him his hair was a silver-grey,
rather longer than it was the fashion to wear,
and his eyes were a deep blue. He was clean
shaven, and, as he walked, always seemed a
little unsteady in his gait. At Oxford he was
a well-known figure. He was a little eccentric
in his clothes. In the coldest weather he
would never wear an overcoat, and he had a
curious habit of always wearing, in all seasons
of the year, a pair of grey and black cotton
gloves.

But for the whiteness of his hair it was
difficult to tell his age from his face, for there
were no wrinkles on it. He had a curiously
womanish face, and, in direct contradiction to
his real character, there seemed to be little
strength in it. One reads a great deal about
the lines that a man's life paints in his face,
and there are many people who believe that
character is indicated by the curves of flesh

and bone. I do not, and never shall, believe it is true, and Lewis Carroll is only one of many instances to support my theory. He was as firm and self-contained as a man may be, but there was little to show it in his face.

Yet you could easily discern it in the way in which he met and talked with his friends. When he shook hands with you—he had firm white hands, rather large—his grip was strong and steadfast. Every one knows the kind of man of whom it is said, "his hands were all soft and flabby when he said 'How-do-you-do.'" Well, Lewis Carroll was not a bit like that. Every one says when he shook your hand the pressure of his was full of strength, and you felt here indeed was a man to admire and to love. The expression in his eyes was also very kind and charming.

He used to look at me, when we met, in the very tenderest, gentlest way. Of course on an ordinary occasion I knew that his interested glance did not mean anything of any extra importance. Nothing could have

happened since I had seen him last, yet,
at the same time, his look was always so
deeply sympathetic and benevolent, that one
could hardly help feeling it meant a great
deal more than the expression of the ordinary
man.

He was afflicted with what I believe is
known as " Housemaid's knee," and this made
his movements singularly jerky and abrupt.
Then again he found it impossible to avoid
stammering in his speech. He would, when
engaged in an animated conversation with a
friend, talk quickly and well for a few minutes,
and then suddenly and without any very
apparent cause would begin to stutter so
much, that it was often difficult to understand
him. He was very conscious of this impedi-
ment, and he tried hard to cure himself. For
several years he read a scene from some play
of Shakespeare's every day aloud, but despite
this he was never quite able to cure himself of the habit. Many people would have
found this a great hindrance to the affairs
of ordinary life, and would have felt it

deeply. Lewis Carroll was different. His mind and life was so simple and open that there was no room in them for self-consciousness, and I have often heard him jest at his own misfortune, with a comic wonder at it.

The personal characteristic that you would notice most on meeting Lewis Carroll was his extreme shyness. With children, of course, he was not nearly so reserved, but in the society of people of maturer age he was almost old-maidishly prim in his manner. When he knew a child well this reserve would vanish completely, but it needed only a slightly disconcerting incident to bring the cloak of shyness about him once more, and close the lips that just before had been talking so delightfully.

I shall never forget one afternoon when we had been walking in Christ Church meadows. On one side of the great open space the little river Cherwell runs through groves of trees towards the Isis, where the college boat-races are rowed. We were going quietly along by the side of the "Cher," when he began to explain to me that the tiny stream was a tributary, "a baby river" he put it, of the big Thames. He talked for some minutes, explaining how rivers came down from hills and flowed eventually to the sea, when he suddenly met a brother Don at a turning in the avenue.

He was holding my hand and giving me my lesson in geography with great earnestness when the other man came round the corner.

He greeted him in answer to his salutation, but the incident disturbed his train of thought, and for the rest of the walk he became very difficult to understand, and talked in a nervous and preoccupied manner. One strange way in which his nervousness affected him was peculiarly characteristic. When, owing to the stupendous success of "Alice in Wonderland" and "Alice Through the Looking-Glass," he became a celebrity, many people were anxious to see him, and in some way or other to find out what manner of man he was. This seemed to him horrible, and he invented a mild deception for use when some autograph-hunter or curious person sent him a request for his signature on a photograph, or asked him some silly question as to the writing of one of his books, how long it took to write, and how many copies had been sold. Through some third person he always represented that Lewis Carroll the author and Mr. Dodgson the professor were two distinct persons, and that the author could not be heard of at Oxford at all. On one occasion an American actually wrote to say that he had heard that Lewis Carroll had laid out a garden to represent some of the scenes in "Alice in Wonderland," and that he (the American) was coming right away to take photographs of it. Poor Lewis Carroll, he was in terror of Americans for a week !

Of being photographed he had a horror, and despite the fact that he was continually and importunately requested to sit before the camera, only very few photographs of

C. L. DODGSON

him are in existence. Yet he had been himself a great amateur photographer, and had taken many pictures that were remarkable in their exact portraiture of the subject.

It was this exactness that he used to pride himself on in his camera work. He always said that modern professional photographers spoilt all their pictures by touching them up absurdly to flatter the sitter. When it was necessary for me to have some pictures taken he sent me to Mr. H. H. Cameron, whom he declared to be the only artist who dared to produce a photograph that was exactly like its subject. I thought that Mr. Cameron's picture made me look a dreadful fright, but Lewis Carroll always declared that it was a perfect specimen of portrait work.

Many of the photographs of children in this book are Lewis Carroll's work. Miss Beatrice Hatch, to whose kindness I am indebted for these photographs and for much interesting information, writes in the *Strand Magazine* (April 1898): "My earliest recollections of Mr. Dodgson are connected with photography. He was very fond of this art at one time, though he had entirely given it up for many years latterly. He kept various costumes and 'properties' with which to dress us up, and, of course, that added to the fun. What child would not thoroughly enjoy personating a Japanese or a beggar child, or a gipsy or an Indian. Sometimes there were excursions to the roof of the college, which was easily accessible from the windows of the studio. Or you might stand by your friend's side in the tiny dark room and watch him while he poured the contents of several little strong-smelling bottles on to the glass picture of yourself that looked so funny with its black face."

Yet, despite his love for the photographer's art, he hated the idea of having his own picture taken for the benefit of a curious world. The shyness that made him nervous in the presence of strangers made the idea that any one who cared to stare into a shop window could examine and criticise his portrait extremely repulsive to him.

I remember that this shyness of his was

A CHINAMAN

the only occasion of anything approaching a quarrel between us.

I had an idle trick of drawing caricatures
when I was a child, and one day when he
was writing some letters I began to make a
picture of him on the back of an envelope.
I quite forget what the drawing was like—
probably it was an abominable libel—but
suddenly he turned round and saw what I
was doing. He got up from his seat and
turned very red, frightening me very much.
Then he took my poor little drawing, and
tearing it into small pieces threw it into the
fire without a word. Afterwards he came
suddenly to me, and saying nothing, caught
me up in his arms and kissed me passionately.
I was only some ten or eleven years of age
at the time, but now the incident comes
back to me very clearly, and I can see it
as if it happened but yesterday—the sudden
snatching of my picture, the hurried strid-
ing across the room, and then the tender light
in his face as he caught me up to him and
kissed me.

I used to see a good deal of him at Oxford,
and I was constantly in Christ Church. He

would invite me to stay with him and find me rooms just outside the college gates, where I was put into charge of an elderly dame, whose name, if I do not forget, was Mrs. Buxall. I would spend long happy days with my uncle, and at nine o'clock I was taken over to the little house in St. Aldates and delivered into the hands of the landlady, who put me to bed.

In the morning I was awakened by the deep reverberations of "Great Tom" calling Oxford to wake and begin the new day. Those times were very pleasant, and the remembrance of them lingers with me still. Lewis Carroll at the time of which I am speaking had two tiny turret rooms, one on each side of his staircase in Christ Church. He always used to tell me that when I grew up and became married he would give me the two little rooms, so that if I ever disagreed with my husband we could each of us retire to a turret till we had made up our quarrel!

And those rooms of his! I do not think

there was ever such a fairy-land for children. I am sure they must have contained one of the finest collections of musical-boxes to be found anywhere in the world. There were big black ebony boxes with glass tops, through which you could see all the works. There was a big box with a handle, which it was quite hard exercise for a little girl to turn, and there must have been twenty or thirty little ones which could only play one tune. Sometimes one of the musical-boxes would not play properly, and then I always got tremendously excited. Uncle used to go to a drawer in the table and produce a box of little screw-drivers and punches, and while I sat on his knee he would unscrew the lid and take out the wheels to see what was the matter. He must have been a clever mechanist, for the result was always the same—after a longer or shorter period the music began again. Sometimes when the musical-boxes had played all their tunes he used to put them into the box backwards, and was as pleased as I at the comic effect of the

music "standing on its head," as he phrased
it.

There was another and very wonderful toy
which he sometimes produced for me, and
this was known as "The Bat." The ceilings
of the rooms in which he lived at the time
were very high indeed, and admirably suited
for the purposes of "The Bat." It was an
ingeniously constructed toy of gauze and wire,
which actually flew about the room like a
bat. It was worked by a piece of twisted
elastic, and it could fly for about half a
minute.

I was always a little afraid of this toy
because it was too lifelike, but there was a
fearful joy in it. When the music-boxes
began to pall he would get up from his
chair and look at me with a knowing smile.
I always knew what was coming even before
he began to speak, and I used to dance up and
down in tremulous anticipation.

"Isa, my darling," he would say, "once
upon a time there was some one called Bob
the Bat! and he lived in the top left-hand

drawer of the writing-table. What could he
do when uncle wound him up?"

And then I would squeak out breathlessly,
" He could really FLY ! "

Bob the Bat had many adventures. There
was no way of controlling the direction of its
flight, and one morning, a hot summer's
morning, when the window was wide open,
Bob flew out into the garden and alighted in
a bowl of salad which a scout was taking to
some one's rooms. The poor fellow was so
startled by the sudden flapping apparition that
he dropped the bowl, and it was broken into
a thousand pieces.

There ! I have written "a thousand pieces,"
and a thoughtless exaggeration of that sort
was a thing that Lewis Carroll hated. " A
thousand pieces ? " he would have said ;
" you know, Isa, that if the bowl had been
broken into a thousand pieces they would
each have been so tiny that you could have
hardly seen them. And if the broken pieces
had been get-at-able, he would have made
me count them as a means of impressing

on my mind the folly of needless exaggeration.

I remember how annoyed he was once when, after a morning's sea bathing at Eastbourne, I exclaimed, " Oh this salt water, it always makes my hair as stiff as a poker."

He impressed it on me quite irritably that no little girl's hair could ever possibly get as stiff as a poker. "If you had said, 'as stiff as wires,' it would have been more like it, but even that would have been an exaggeration." And then, seeing that I was a little frightened, he drew for me a picture of "The little girl called Isa whose hair turned into pokers because she was always exaggerating things."

That and all the other pictures that he drew for me are, I'm sorry to say, the sole property of the little fishes in the Irish Channel, where a clumsy porter dropped them as we hurried into the boat at Holyhead.

"I nearly died of laughing," was another expression that he particularly disliked ; in fact any form of exaggeration generally called from

him a reproof, though he was sometimes con-
tent to make fun. For instance, my sisters
and I had sent him " millions of kisses " in
a letter. Below you will find the letter that
he wrote in return, written in the violet ink
that he always used (dreadfully ugly, I used to
think it).

Ch. Ch. Oxford
Ap. 14. 1890.

My own Darling,

It's all very well for you
& Nellie & Emsie to unite in
millions of hugs & kisses, but
please consider the time it
would occupy your poor old
very busy Uncle! Try hugging
& kissing Emsie for a minute
by the watch, & I don't think
you'll manage it more than
20 times a minute. "Millions"
must mean 2 millions at least

20)2,000,000 hugs & kisses
   60)100,000 minutes
      12)1,666 hours
         6)138 days [at 12 hours a day
            23 weeks.

I couldn't go on hugging &
kissing more than 12 hours a
day. & I wouldn't like to spend
Sundays that way. So you see
it would take 23 weeks of

hard work. Really, my dear Child, I cannot spare the time.

Why haven't I written since my last letter? Why, how could I, you silly silly Child? How could I have written since the last time I did write? Now, you just try it with kissing. Go & kiss Nellie, from me, several times, And take care to manage it so as to have kissed her since the last time" you did kiss her. Now go back to your place, & I'll question you.

"Have you kissed her several times?"

"Yes, darling Uncle"

"What o'clock was it when you gave her the last kiss?"

"5 minutes past 10, Uncle"

"Very well. Now, have you kissed her since?"

"Well —— I —— ahem ahem! ahem! (Excuse me, Uncle, I've got a bad cough)

I —— thinks —— that —— I
—— that is, you, know, I —— "
"Yes, I see! "Isa" begins with
'I', and it seems to me as if she
was going to end with 'I', this time!"
Anyhow, my not writing
hasn't been because I was ill,
but because I was a horrid lazy
old thing, who kept putting
it off from day to day, till
at last I said to myself
"Who roar! There's no time to
write now, because they sail
on the 1st of April". In fact,
I shouldn't have been a bit
surprised if this letter had been
from Fulham, instead of
Louisville. Well, I suppose
you will be there by about the
middle of May. But mind
you don't write to me from
there! Please, please, no more
horrid letters from you! I do
hate them so! And as for kissing
them when I get them, why, I'd
just as soon kiss —— kiss —

kiss you, you tiresome thing!
So there now!

Thank you very much for
those 2 photographs. I liked
them —— hum —— pretty well.
I can't honestly say I thought
them the very best I had ever
seen.

Please give my kindest
regards to your mother, and
$\frac{1}{2}$ of a kiss to Nellie, & $\frac{1}{200}$
of a kiss to Emsie, & $\frac{1}{2000000}$
of a kiss to yourself.

So, with fondest love, I am,
my darling, your loving Uncle,
C. L. Dodgson

P.S. I've thought about that
little prayer you asked me to
write for Nellie & Emsie. But I
would like, first, to have the
words of the one I wrote for you,
& the words of what they now say,
if they say any. And then I will
pray to our Heavenly Father to
help me to write a prayer that
will be really fit for them to use.

"CH. CH. OXFORD.
Ap. 14, 1890.

"MY OWN DARLING,

"It's all very well for you and Nellie and Emsie to write in million of hugs and kisses, but please consider the *time* it would occupy your poor old very busy Uncle! Try hugging and kissing Emsie for a minute by the watch, and I don't think you'll manage it more than 20 times a minute. 'Millions' must mean 2 millions at least.

```
20)2,000,000 hugs and kisses
60)100,000 minutes
12)1,666 hours
6)138 days (at twelve hours a day)
23 weeks.
```

"I couldn't go on hugging and kissing more than 12 hours a day: and I wouldn't like to spend *Sundays* that way. So you see it would take 23 *weeks* of hard work. Really, my dear child, *I cannot spare the time.*

"Why haven't I written since my last letter? Why, how *could* I, you silly little child? How could I have written *since the last time* I *did* write? Now, you just try it with kissing. Go and kiss Nellie, from me, several times, and take care to manage it so as to have kissed her *since the last time* you *did* kiss her. Now go back to your place and I'll question you.

" ' Have you kissed her several times? '

" ' Yes, darling Uncle.'

" ' What o'clock was it when you gave her the *last* kiss? '

" ' 5 minutes past 10, Uncle.'

" ' Very well, now, have you kissed her *since*? '

" ' Well—I—ahem! ahem! ahem! (excuse me, Uncle, I've got a bad cough). I—think that—I—that is, you, know I——— '

" ' Yes, I see! Isa begins with " I," and it seems to me as if she was going to *end* it with " I " *this* time! '

"Anyhow, my not writing hasn't been because I was *ill*, but because I was a horrid lazy old thing, who kept putting it off from day to day till at last I said to myself, 'UHO ROAR! There's no time to write now, because they *sail* on the 1st of April.'[1] In fact, I shouldn't have been a bit surprised if this letter had been from *Fulham*, instead of Louisville. Well, I suppose you *will* be there about the middle of May. But mind you don't write to me from there ! Please, please, no more horrid letters from you ! I *do* hate them so ! And as for *kissing* them when I get them, why, I'd just as soon kiss—kiss—kiss *you*, you tiresome thing ! So there now !

"Thank you very much for those two photographs—I liked them—hum—pretty well. I can't, however, say that I thought them the best I had ever seen.

"Please give my kindest regards to your mother, and $\frac{1}{2}$ of a kiss to Nelly, and $\frac{1}{200}$ of a kiss to Emsie, and $\frac{1}{2,000,000}$ of a kiss to yourself. So, with fondest love, I am, my darling, your loving Uncle,

"C. L. Dodgson."

[1] This refers to my visit to America when, as a child, I played the little Duke of York in "Richard III."

And now, in the postscript, comes one of
the rare instances in which Lewis Carroll showed
his deep religious feeling.   It runs—

" *P.S.*—I've thought about that little prayer
you asked me to write for Nellie and Emsie.
But I would like, first, to have the words of
the one I wrote for *you*, and the words of
what they *now* say, if they say any.   And
then I will pray to Our Heavenly Father to
help me to write a prayer that will be really
fit for them to use."

Again, I had ended one of my letters with
"all join me in lufs and kisses."   It was a
letter written when I was away from home
and alone, and I had put the usual ending
thoughtlessly and in haste, for there was no
one that I knew in all that town who could
have joined me in my messages to him.   He
answered me as follows :—

"7 LUSHINGTON ROAD, EASTBOURNE,
Aug. 30, 90.

"Oh, you naughty, naughty, bad wicked
little girl!   You forgot to put a stamp on

your letter, and your poor old uncle had to pay
TWOPENCE !   His *last* Twopence !   Think
of that.   I shall punish you severely for this
when once I get you here.   So *tremble* !   Do
you hear ?   Be good enough to tremble !

"I've only time for one question to-day.
Who in the world are the 'all' that join you
in 'Lufs and kisses.'   Weren't you fancying
you were at home, and sending messages (as
people constantly do) from Nellie and Emsie
without their having given any ?   It isn't a
good plan that sending messages people haven't
given.   I don't mean it's in the least *untruth-
ful*, because everybody knows how commonly
they are sent without having been given ; but
it lessens the pleasure of receiving the messages.
My sisters write to me 'with best love from
all.'   I know it isn't true ; so I don't value it
much.   The other day, the husband of one of
my 'child-friends' (who always writes 'your
loving') wrote to me and ended with 'Ethel
joins me in kindest regards.'   In my answer I
said (of course in fun)—'I am not going to
send Ethel kindest regards, so I won't send her

any message *at all.*' Then she wrote to say
she didn't even know he was writing ! 'Of
course I would have sent best love,' and she
added that she had given her husband a piece
of her mind ! Poor husband !

"Your always loving uncle,

"C. L. D."

These letters are written in Lewis Carroll's
ordinary handwriting, not a particularly legible
one. When, however, he was writing for the
press no characters could have been more
clearly and distinctly formed than his.
Throughout his life he always made it his
care to give as little trouble as possible to
other people. "Why should the printers have
to work overtime because my letters are ill-
formed and my words run into each other ?" he
once said, when a friend remonstrated with him
because he took such pains with the writing
of his "copy." As a specimen of his careful
penmanship the diary that he wrote for me,
which is reproduced in this book in facsimile,
is an admirable example.

They were happy days, those days in Oxford, spent with the most fascinating companion that a child could have. In our walks about the old town, in our visits to cathedral or chapel or hall, in our visits to his friends he was an ideal companion, but I think I was almost happiest when we came back to his rooms and had tea alone; when the fire-glow (it was always winter when I stayed in Oxford) threw fantastic shadows about the quaint room, and the thoughts of the prosiest of people must have wandered a little into fancy-land. The shifting firelight seemed to almost æthere-alise that kindly face, and as the wonderful stories fell from his lips, and his eyes lighted on me with the sweetest smile that ever a man wore, I was conscious of a love and reverence for Charles Dodgson that became nearly an adoration.

It was almost pain when the lights were turned up and we came back to everyday life and tea.

He was very particular about his tea, which he always made himself, and in order that it should draw properly he would walk about the room swinging the tea-pot from side to side for exactly ten minutes. The idea of the grave professor promenading his book-lined study and carefully waving a teapot to and fro may seem ridiculous, but all the minutiæ of life received an extreme attention at his hands, and after the first surprise one came quickly to realise the convenience that his carefulness ensured.

Before starting on a railway journey, for instance (and how delightful were railway journeys in the company of Lewis Carroll), he used to map out exactly every minute of the time that we were to take on the way. The details of the journey completed, he would exactly calculate the amount of money that must be spent, and, in different partitions of the two purses that he carried, arrange the various sums that would be necessary for cabs, porters, newspapers, refreshments, and the other expenses of a journey. It was wonderful how much trouble he saved himself *en route* by thus making ready beforehand. Lewis

Carroll was never driven half frantic on a

BEGGAR CHILDREN

station platform because he had to change

sovereign to buy a penny paper while the
train was on the verge of starting. With him
journeys were always comfortable.

Of the joys that waited on a little girl who
stayed with Lewis Carroll at his Oxford home
I can give no better idea than that furnished
by the diary that follows, which he wrote for
me, bit by bit, during the evenings of one of
my stays at Oxford.

Isa's Visit to Oxford.
1888.

Chap. I.

On wednesday, the Eleventh of
July, Isa happened to meet a friend
at Paddington Station at half-past-
-ten. She can't remember his name, but
she says he was an old old old gentleman,
and he had invited her, she thinks, to
go with him somewhere or other, she can't
remember where.

Chap. II.

The first thing they did, after calling
at a shop, was to go to the Panorama
of the "Falls of Niagara". Isa thought
it very wonderful. You seemed to be on
the top of a tower, with miles and miles
of country all round you. The things
in front were real, and somehow they
joined into the picture behind, so that

you couldn't tell where the real things
ended and the picture began - Near the
foot of the Falls, there was a steam-packet
crossing the river, which showed what a
tremendous height the Falls must be, it
looked so tiny. In the road in front were
two men and a dog, standing looking the
other way - They may have been wooden
figures, or part of the picture, there was
no knowing which. The man, who stood
next to Isa, said to another man "That
dog looked round just now. Now see, I'll
whistle to him, and make him look round
again!" And he began whistling: and Isa
almost expected, it looked so exactly
like a real dog, that it would turn its
head to see who was calling it!

After that Isa and her friend (the
Aged Aged Man) went to the house of a
Mr Dymes - Mrs Dymes gave them some
dinner, and two of her children, called
Helen and Maud, went with them to

Terry's Theatre, to see the play of "Little Lord Fauntleroy". Little Véra Beringer was the little Lord Fauntleroy. Isa would have liked to play the part, but the Manager at the Theatre did not allow her, as she did not know the words, which would have made it go off badly. Isa liked the whole play very much : the passionate old Earl, and the gentle Mother of the little boy, and the droll "Mr. Hobbs", and all of them.

Then they all went off by the Metro-politan Railway, and the two Miss Dymeses got out at their station, and Isa and the A.A.M. went on to Oxford. A kind old lady called Mrs Symonds, had invited Isa to come and sleep at her house : and she was soon fast asleep, and dreaming that she and little Lord Fauntleroy were going in a steamer down the Falls of Niagara, and whistling to a dog, who was in such a hurry to go up the Falls that he wouldn't attend to them.

Chap. III

,The next morning Isa set off,
almost before she was awake, with the
A.A.M., to pay a visit to a little College,
called "Christ Church". You go in under
a magnificent tower, called "Tom Tower",
nearly four feet high (so that Isa had
hardly to stoop at all, to go under it) into
the Great Quadrangle (which very vulgar
people call "Tom Quad".) You should always
be polite, even when speaking to a
Quadrangle: it might seem not to take
any notice, but it doesn't like being
called names. On their way to Christ Church
they saw a tall monument, like the spire
of a church, called the "Martyrs' Memo-
rial", put up in memory of three Bishops,
Cranmer, Ridley, and Latimer, who
were burned in the reign of Queen Mary,
because they would not be Roman Catho-
-lics. Christ Church was built in 1546.

They had breakfast at Ch. Ch., in
the rooms of the A.A.M., and then Isa

learned how to print with the "Type-
Writer", and printed several beautiful
volumes of poetry, all of her own in-
-vention — By this time it was 1 o'clock,
so Isa paid a visit to the Kitchen, to
make sure that the chicken, for her
dinner, was being properly roasted. The
Kitchen is about the oldest part of the
College, so was built about 1546. It
has a fire-grate large enough to roast
forty legs of mutton at once.

Then they saw the Dining Hall, in
which the A.A.M. has dined several times,
(about 8000 times, perhaps). After
dinner, they went, through the Quadrangle
of the Bodleian Library, into Broad Street.
and, as a band was just going by, of
course they followed it. (Isa likes
Bands better than anything in the world,
except Lands, and walking on Sands,
and wringing her Hands). The Band
led them into the gardens of Wadham
College (built in 1613), where there was

a school-treat going on. The treat was,
first marching twice round the garden—
then having a photograph done of them all
in a row —— then a *promise* of "Punch
and Judy", which wouldn't be ready for
20 minutes, so Isa, and Co., wouldn't
wait, but went back to Ch. Ch., and saw
the "Broad Walk". In the evening they
played at "Reversi", till Isa had lost
the small remainder of her temper.
Then she went to bed, and dreamed she
was Judy, and was beating Punch with
a stick of barley-sugar.

Chap. IV.

On Friday morning (after taking
her medicine very amiably), went
with the A.A.M. (who *would* go with
her, though she told him over and over
she would rather be alone) to the gardens
of Worcester College (built in 1714)
where they didn't see the swans (who
ought to have been on the lake), nor the

hippopotamus, who ought not to have
been walking about among the flowers,
gathering honey like a busy bee.

After breakfast Isa helped the
A..A.M. to pack his luggage, because he
thought he would go away, he didn't know
where, some day, he didn't know when—
So she put a lot of things, she didn't know
what, into boxes, she didn't know which.

After dinner they went to St. John's
College (built in 1555), and admired
the large lawn, where more than 150
ladies, dressed in robes of gold and
silver, were not walking about.

Then they saw the Chapel of Keble
College (built in 1870) = and then the
New Museum, where Isa quite lost her
heart to a charming stuffed Gorilla,
that smiled on her from a glass case.
The Museum was finished in 1860.
The most curious thing they saw there
was a "Walking Leaf", a kind of insect

that looks exactly like a withered leaf.

Then they went to New College (built in 1386), & saw, close to the entrance, a "skew" arch (going slantwise through the wall) one of the first ever built in England. After seeing the gardens, they returned to Ch. Ch. (Parts of the old City walls run round the gardens of New College: and you may still see some of the old narrow slits, through which the defenders could shoot arrows at the attacking army, who could hardly succeed in shooting through them from the outside).

They had tea with Mrs Paget, wife of Dr. Paget one of the Canons of Ch.Ch. Then, after a sorrowful evening, Isa went to bed, and dreamed she was buzzing about among the flowers, with the dear Gorilla: but there wasn't any honey in them — only slices of bread-and-butter, and multiplication-tables

Chap. V.

On Saturday Isa had a Music Lesson, and learned to play on an American Orguinette. It is not a very difficult instrument to play, as you only have to turn a handle round and round: so she did it nicely. You put a long piece of paper in, and it goes through the machine, and the holes in the paper make different notes play. They put one in wrong end first, and had a tune backwards, and soon found themselves in the day before yesterday: So they dared not go on, for fear of making Isa so young she would not be able to talk. The A.A.M. does not like visitors who only howl, and get red in the face, from morning to night.

In the afternoon they went round Ch. Ch. meadow, and saw the Barges, belonging to the Colleges, and some pretty views of Magdalen Tower through the trees -

LEWIS CARROLL 49

Then they went through the "Botanical
Gardens, built in the year —— no, by
the bye, they never were built at all. And
then to Magdalen College. At the top of the
wall, in one corner, they saw a very large
jolly face, carved in stone, with a broad
grin, and a little man at the side, helping
him to laugh by pulling up the corner of his
mouth for him. Isa thought that, the next
time she wants to laugh, she will get Nellie
and Maggie to help her — With two people to
pull up the corners of your mouth for you,
it is as easy to laugh as can be!

They went into Magdalen Meadow, which
has a pretty walk all round it, arched over
with trees: and there they met a lady "from
Amurrica," as she told them, who wanted to
know the way to "Addison's Walk," and par-
-ticularly wanted to know if there would be
"any danger" in going there. They told her the
way, and that <u>most</u> of the lions and tigers
and buffaloes, round the meadow, were quite
gentle and hardly ever killed people: so
she set off, pale and trembling, and they

saw her no more : only they heard her
screams in the distance; so they guessed
what had happened to her.

Then they rode in a tram-car to another
part of Oxford, and called on a lady called
Mrs Jeune, and her little grand-daughter,
called "Noël", because she was born on
Christmas-Day _ ("Noël" is the French name
for "Christmas".) And there they had so
much Tea that at last Isa nearly turned
into "Teaser".

Then they went home, down a little
narrow street, where there was a little
dog standing fixed in the middle of the
street, as if its feet were glued to the
ground : they asked it how long it meant to
stand there, and it said (as well as it
could) "till the week after next".

Then Isa went to bed, and dreamed
she was going round Magdalen Meadow,
with the "Amurrican" lady, and there
was a buffalo sitting at the top of every
tree, handing her cups of tea as she
went underneath : but they all held

the cups upside-down, so that the tea
poured all over her head and ran down
her face.

Chap. VI

On Sunday morning they went
to St. Mary's church, in High Street.
In coming home, down the street next
to the one where they had found a fixed
dog, they found a fixed cat — a poor
little kitten, that had put out its head
through the bars of the cellar-window,
and get back again. They rang the bell
at the next door, but the maid said the
cellar wasn't in that house, and, before
they could get to the right door the cat
had unfixed its head — either from
its neck or from the bars, and had gone
inside. Isa thought the animals in
this city have a curious way of fixing
themselves up and down the place, as
if they were hat-pegs.

Then they went back to Ch. Ch., and
looked at a lot of dresses, which

the A.A.M. kept in a cupboard, to dress up children in, when they come to be photo-graphed. Some of the dresses had been used in Pantomimes at Drury Lane: some were rags, to dress up beggar-children in: some had been very magnificent once, but were getting quite old and shabby. Talking of old dresses, there is one College in Ox-ford, so old that it is not known for certain when it was built. The people, who live there, say it was built more than 1000 years ago: and, when they say this, the people who live in the other Colleges never contradict them, but listen most respectfully —— only they wink a little with one eye, as if they didn't quite believe it.

The same day, Isa saw a curious book of pictures of ghosts. If you look hard at one for a minute, and then look at the ceiling, you see another ghost there: only, when you have a black one in the book, it is a white one on the

ceiling : when it is green in the book,
it is _pink_ on the ceiling.

In the middle of the day, as usual,
Isa had her dinner : but this time it
was grander than usual. There was a
dish of "Meringues" (this is pronounced
"Marangs"), which Isa thought so good
that she would have liked to live on them
all the rest of her life.

They took a little walk in the after-
-noon, and in the middle of Broad Street
they saw a cross buried in the ground,
very near the place where the Martyrs
were burned. Then they went into the
gardens of Trinity College (built in
1554) to see the "Lime Walk", a pretty
little avenue of lime-trees. The great
iron "gates" at the end of the garden
are not real gates, but all done in one
piece : and they couldn't open them, even
if you knocked all day. Isa thought them
a miserable sham.

Then they went into the "Parks" (this word doesn't mean "parks, of grass, with trees and deer," but "parks" of guns: that is, great rows of cannons, which stood there when King Charles the First was in Oxford, and Oliver Cromwell fighting against him.

They saw "Mansfield College", a new College just begun to be built, with such tremendously narrow windows that Isa was afraid the young gentle -men who come there will not be able to see to learn their lessons, and will go away from Oxford just as wise as they came.

Then they went to the evening ser -vice at New College, and heard some beautiful singing and organ-playing. Then back to Ch. Ch., in pouring rain. Isa tried to count the drops: but, when she had counted four millions, three hundred and seventy-eight thousand, two hundred and forty-seven, she got tired of counting, and left off.

    After dinner, Isa got somebody or other (she is not sure who it was) to finish this story for her. Then she went to bed, and dreamed she was fixed in the middle of Oxford, with her feet fast to the ground, and her head between the bars of a cellar-window, in a sort of final tableau. Then she dreamed the curtain came down, and the people all called out "encore!" But she cried out "Oh, not again! It would be too dreadful to have my visit all over again!" But, on second thoughts, she smiled in her sleep, and said "Well, do you know, after all, I think I wouldn't mind so very much if I did have it all over again!".

Lewis Carroll.

THE END

This diary, and what I have written before, show how I, as a little girl, knew Lewis Carroll at Oxford.

For his little girl friends, of course, he reserved the most intimate side of his nature, but on occasion he would throw off his reserve and talk earnestly and well to some young man in whose life he took an interest.

Mr. Arthur Girdlestone is able to bear witness to this, and he has given me an account of an evening that he once spent with Lewis Carroll, which I reproduce here from notes made during our conversation.

Mr. Girdlestone, then an undergraduate at New College, had on one occasion to call on Lewis Carroll at his rooms in Tom Quad. At the time of which I am speaking Lewis Carroll had retired very much from the society which he had affected a few years before. Indeed for the last years of his life he was almost a recluse, and beyond dining in Hall saw hardly any one. Miss Beatrice Hatch, one of his "girl friends," writes apropos of his hermit-like seclusion :—

"If you were very anxious to get him to come to your house on any particular day, the only chance was *not* to *invite* him, but only to inform him that you would be at home. Otherwise he would say, 'As you have *invited* me I cannot come, for I have made a rule to decline all *invitations*; but I will come the next day.' In former years he would sometimes consent to go to a 'party' if he was quite sure he was not to be 'shown off' or introduced to any one as the author of 'Alice.' I must again quote from a note of his in answer to an invitation to tea: 'What an awful proposition! To drink tea from four to six would tax the constitution even of a hardened tea drinker! For me, who hardly ever touch it, it would probably be fatal.'"

All through the University, except in an extremely limited circle, Lewis Carroll was regarded as a person who lived very much by himself. "When," Mr. Girdlestone said to me, "I went to see him on quite a slight acquaintance, I confess it was with some slight feeling of trepidation. However I had to go on some business, and accordingly I knocked at his door about 8.30 one winter's evening, and was invited to come in.

"He was sitting working at a writing-table, and all round him were piles of MSS. arranged with mathematical neatness, and many of them tied up with tape. The lamp threw his face into sharp relief as he greeted me. My business was soon over, and I was about to go away, when he asked me if I would have a glass of wine and sit with him for a little.

"The night outside was very cold, and the fire was bright and inviting, and I sat down. He began to talk to me of ordinary subjects, of the things a man might do at Oxford, of the place itself, and the affection in which he held it. He talked quietly, and in a rather tired voice. During our conversation my eye fell upon a photograph of a little girl— evidently from the freshness of its appearance but newly taken—which was resting upon the ledge of a reading-stand at my elbow. It was the picture of a tiny child, very pretty, and I picked it up to look at it.

"'That is the baby of a girl friend of mine,' he said, and then, with an absolute change of voice, 'there is something very strange about very young children, something I cannot understand.' I asked him in what way, and he explained at some length. He was far less at his ease than when talking trivialities, and he occasionally stammered and sometimes hesitated for a word. I cannot remember all he said, but some of his remarks still remain with me. He said that in the company of very little children his brain enjoyed a rest which was startlingly recuperative. If he had been working too hard or had tired his brain in any way, to play with children was like an actual material tonic to his whole system. I understood him to say that the effect was almost physical!

"He said that he found it much easier to understand children, to get his mind into correspondence with their minds when he was fatigued with other work. Personally, I did not understand little children, and they seemed quite outside my experience, and rather incautiously I asked him if children never bored him. He had been standing up for most of the time, and when I asked him that, he sat down suddenly. 'They are three-fourths of my life,' he said. 'I cannot understand how any one could be bored by little children. I think when you are older you will come to see this—I hope you'll come to see it.'

"After that he changed the subject once more, and became again the mathematician—a little formal, and rather weary."

Mr. Girdlestone probably had a unique experience, for it was but rarely that Mr. Dodgson so far unburdened himself to a comparative stranger, and what was even worse, to a " grown-up stranger."

Now I have given you two different phases of Lewis Carroll at Oxford—Lewis Carroll as the little girl's companion, and Lewis Carroll sitting by the fireside telling something of his inner self to a young man. I am going on to talk about my life with him at Eastbourne, where I used, year by year, to stay with him at his house in Lushington Road.

ST. GEORGE AND THE DRAGON

He was very fond of Eastbourne, and it was from that place that I received the most charming letters that he wrote me. Here is one, and I could hardly say how many times I have taken this delightful letter from its drawer to read through and through again.

"7 LUSHINGTON ROAD, EASTBOURNE,
September 17, 1893.

"Oh, you naughty, naughty little culprit! If only I could fly to Fulham with a handy little stick (ten feet long and four inches thick is my favourite size) how I would rap your wicked little knuckles. However, there isn't much harm done, so I will sentence you to a very mild punishment — only one year's imprisonment. If you'll just tell the Fulham policeman about it, he'll manage all the rest for you, and he'll fit you with a nice comfortable pair of handcuffs, and lock you up in a nice cosy dark cell, and feed you on nice dry bread and delicious cold water.

"But how badly you *do* spell your words! I *was* so puzzled about the 'sacks full of love and baskets full of kisses!' But at last I made out why, of course, you meant 'a sack full of *gloves*, and a basket full of *kittens!*' Then I understood what you were sending me. And just then Mrs. Dyer came to tell me a large sack and a basket had come. There was such a miawing in the house, as if all the cats in Eastbourne had come to see me! 'Oh, just open them please, Mrs. Dyer, and count the things in them!'

"So in a few minutes Mrs. Dyer came and said, '500 pairs of gloves in the sack and 250 kittens in the basket.'

"'Dear me! That makes 1000 gloves! four times as many gloves as kittens! It's very kind of Maggie, but why did she send so many gloves? for I haven't got 1000 *hands*, you know, Mrs. Dyer.'

"And Mrs. Dyer said, 'No, indeed, you're 998 hands short of that!'

"However the next day I made out what to do, and I took the basket with me and walked off to the parish school—the *girls'* school, you know—and I said to the mistress,

' How many little girls are there at school
to-day?'

"'Exactly 250, sir.'

"'And have they all been *very* good all
day?'

"'As good as gold, sir.'

"So I waited outside the door with my
basket, and as each little girl came out, I just
popped a soft little kitten into her hands!
Oh what joy there was! The little girls went
all dancing home, nursing their kittens, and
the whole air was full of purring! Then, the
next morning, I went to the school, before it
opened, to ask the little girls how the kittens
had behaved in the night. And they all
arrived sobbing and crying, and their faces and
hands were all covered with scratches, and
they had the kittens wrapped up in their
pinafores to keep them from scratching any
more. And they sobbed out, 'The kittens
have been scratching us all night, all the
night.'

"So then I said to myself, 'What a nice
little girl Maggie is. *Now* I see why she

sent all those gloves, and why there are four times as many gloves as kittens!' and I said loud to the little girls, 'Never mind, my dear children, do your lessons *very* nicely, and don't cry any more, and when school is over, you'll find me at the door, and you shall see what you shall see!'

"So, in the evening, when the little girls came running out, with the kittens still wrapped up in their pinafores, there was I, at the door, with a big sack! And, as each little girl came out, I just popped into her hand two pairs of gloves! And each little girl unrolled her pinafore and took out an angry little kitten, spitting and snarling, with its claws sticking out like a hedgehog. But it hadn't time to scratch, for, in one moment, it found all its four claws popped into nice soft warm gloves! And then the kittens got quite sweet-tempered and gentle, and began purring again!

"So the little girls went dancing home again, and the next morning they came dancing back to school. The scratches were all healed, and they told me 'The kittens *have* been good!' And, when any kitten wants to catch a mouse, it just takes off *one* of its gloves; and if it wants to catch *two* mice, it takes off two gloves; and if it wants to catch *three* mice, it takes off *three* gloves; and if it wants to catch *four* mice, it takes off all its gloves. But the moment they've caught the mice, they pop their gloves on again, because they know we can't love them without their gloves. For, you see 'gloves' have got 'love' *inside* them—there's none *outside!*'

"So all the little girls said, 'Please thank Maggie, and we send her 250 *loves*, and 1000 *kisses* in return for her 250 kittens and her 1000 *loves!!*' And I told them in the wrong order! and they said they hadn't.

"Your loving old Uncle,

"C. L. D.

"Love and kisses to Nellie and Emsie."

This letter takes up eight pages of close writing, and I should very much doubt if any child ever had a more charming one from anybody. The whimsical fancy in it, the absolute comprehension of a child's intellect, the quickness with which the writer employs the slightest incident or thing that would be likely to please a little girl, is simply wonderful. I shall never forget how the letter charmed and delighted my sister Maggie and myself. We called it "The glove and kitten letter," and as I look at the tremulous handwriting which is lying by my side, it all comes back to me very vividly—like the sound of forgotten fingers on the latch to some lonely fireside watcher, when the wind is wailing round the house with a wilder inner note than it has in the daytime.

At Eastbourne I was happier even with Lewis Carroll than I was at Oxford. We seemed more free, and there was the air of holiday over it all. Every day of my stay at the house in Lushington Road was a perfect dream of delight.

There was one regular and fixed routine which hardly ever varied, and which I came to know by heart; and I will write an account of it here, and ask any little girl who reads it, if she ever had such a splendid time in her life.

To begin with, we used to get up very early indeed. Our bedroom doors faced each other at the top of the staircase. When I came out of mine I always knew if I might go into his room or not by his signal. If, when I came into the passage, I found that a newspaper had been put under the door, then I knew I might go in at once; but if there was no newspaper, then I had to wait till it appeared. I used to sit down on the top stair as quiet as a mouse, watching for the paper to come under the door, when I would rush in almost before uncle had time to get out of the way. This was always the first pleasure and excitement of the day. Then we used to go downstairs to breakfast, after which we always read a chapter out of the Bible. So that I should remember it, I always had to tell it to him afterwards as a story of my own.

LEWIS CARROLL'S HOUSE AT EASTBOURNE

"Now then, Isa dearest," he would say, "tell me a story, and mind you begin with 'once upon a time.' A story which does not begin with 'once upon a time' can't possibly be a good story. It's *most* important."

When I had told my story it was time to go out.

I was learning swimming at the Devonshire Park baths, and we always had a bargain together. He would never allow me to go to the swimming-bath—which I revelled in—until I had promised him faithfully that I would go afterwards to the dentist's.

He had great ideas upon the importance of a regular and almost daily visit to the dentist. He himself went to a dentist as he would have gone to a hairdresser's, and he insisted that all the little girls he knew should go too. The precaution sounds strange, and one might be inclined to think that Lewis Carroll carried it to an unnecessary length; but I can only bear personal witness to the fact that I have firm strong teeth, and have never had a toothache in my life. I believe I owe this

entirely to those daily visits to the Eastbourne
dentist.

Soon after this it was time for lunch, and
we both went back hand-in-hand to the rooms
in Lushington Road. Lewis Carroll never had
a proper lunch, a fact which always used to
puzzle me tremendously.

I could not understand how a big grown-up
man could live on a glass of sherry and a
biscuit at dinner time. It seemed such a pity
when there was lots of mutton and rice-
pudding that he should not have any. I
always used to ask him, "Aren't you hungry,
uncle, even *to-day*."

After lunch I used to have a lesson in back-
gammon, a game of which he was passionately
fond, and of which he could never have enough.
Then came what to me was the great trial of
the day. I am afraid I was a very lazy little
girl in those days, and I know I hated walking
far. The trial was, that we should walk to
the top of Beachy Head every afternoon. I
used to like it very much when I got there,
but the walk was irksome. Lewis Carroll

believed very much in a great amount of exercise, and said one should always go to bed physically wearied with the exercise of the day. Accordingly there was no way out of it, and every afternoon I had to walk to the top of Beachy Head. He was very good and kind. He would invent all sorts of new games to beguile the tedium of the way. One very curious and strange trait in his character was shown on these walks. I used to be very fond of flowers and of animals also. A pretty dog or a hedge of honeysuckle were always pleasant events upon a walk to me. And yet he himself cared for neither flowers nor animals. Tender and kind as he was, simple and unassuming in all his tastes, yet he did not like flowers! I confess that even now I find it hard to understand. He knew children so thoroughly and well—perhaps better than any one else—that it is all the stranger that he did not care for things that generally attract them so much. However, be that as it may, the fact remained. When I was in raptures over a poppy or a dogrose, he would try hard to be

as interested as I was, but even to my childish
eyes it was an obvious effort, and he would
always rather invent some new game for us
to play at.   Once, and once only, I remember
him to have taken an interest in a flower,
and that was because of the folk-lore that was
attached to it, and not because of the beauty
of the flower itself.

We used to walk into the country that
stretched, in beautiful natural avenues of trees,
inland from Eastbourne.   One day while we
sat under a great tree, and the hum of
the myriad insect life rivalled the murmur
of the far-away waves, he took a foxglove
from the heap that lay in my lap and told
me the story of how they came by their name ;
how, in the old days, when, all over England,
there were great forests, like the forest of
Arden that Shakespeare loved, the pixies, the
" little folks," used to wander at night in the
glades, like Titania, and Oberon, and Puck,
and because they took great pride in their
dainty hands they made themselves gloves
out of the flowers.   So the particular flower

that the "little folks" used came to be
called "folks' gloves." Then, because the
country people were rough and clumsy in
their talk, the name was shortened into
"Fox-gloves," the name that every one uses
now.

When I got very tired we used to sit down
upon the grass, and he used to show me the
most wonderful things made out of his handkerchief. Every one when a child has, I
suppose, seen the trick in which a handkerchief
is rolled up to look like a mouse, and then
made to jump about by a movement of the
hand. He did this better than any one I ever
saw, and the trick was a never-failing joy. By
a sort of consent between us the handkerchief
trick was kept especially for the walk to Beachy
Head, when, about half-way, I was a little tired
and wanted to rest. When we actually got to
the Head there was tea waiting in the coastguard's cottage. He always said I ate far
too much, and he would never allow me more
than one rock cake and a cup of tea. This
was an invariable rule, and much as I wished

for it, I was never allowed to have more than one rock cake.

It was in the coastguard's house or on the grass outside that I heard most of his stories. Sometimes he would make excursions into the realms of pure romance, where there were scaly dragons and strange beasts that sat up and talked. In all these stories there was always an adventure in a forest, and the great scene of each tale always took place in a wood. The consummation of a story was always heralded by the phrase, "The children now came to a deep dark wood." When I heard that sentence, which was always spoken very slowly and with a solemn dropping of the voice, I always knew that the really exciting part was coming. I used to nestle a little nearer to him, and he used to hold me a little closer as he told of the final adventure.

He did not always tell me fairy tales, though I think I liked the fairy tales much the best. Sometimes he gave me accounts of adventures which had happened to him. There was one particularly thrilling story of how he was lost on Beachy Head in a sea fog, and had to find his way home by means of boulders. This was the more interesting because we were on the actual scene of the disaster, and to be there stimulated the imagination.

The summer afternoons on the great headland were very sweet and peaceful. I have never met a man so sensible to the influences of Nature as Lewis Carroll. When the sunset was very beautiful he was often affected by the sight. The widespread wrinkled sea below, in the mellow melancholy light of the afternoon, seemed to fit in with his temperament. I have still a mental picture that I can recall of him on the cliff. Just as the sun was setting, and a cool breeze whispered round us, he would take off his hat and let the wind play with his hair, and he would look out to sea. Once I saw tears in his eyes, and when we turned to go he gripped my hand much tighter than usual.

We generally got back to dinner about seven or earlier. He would never let me change my frock for the meal, even if we

were going to a concert or theatre afterwards.
He had a curious theory that a child should
not change her clothes twice in one day.   He
himself made no alteration in his dress at
dinner time, nor would he permit me to do
so.   Yet he was not by any means an untidy
or slovenly man.   He had many little fads
in dress, but his great horror and abomination
was high-heeled shoes with pointed toes.   No
words were strong enough, he thought, to
describe such monstrous things.

Lewis Carroll was a deeply religious man,
and on Sundays at Eastbourne we always went
twice to church.   Yet he held that no child
should be forced into church-going against its
will.   Such a state of mind in a child, he said,
needed most careful treatment, and the very
worst thing to do was to make attendance at
the services compulsory.   Another habit of
his, which must, I feel sure, sound rather
dreadful to many, was that, should the sermon
prove beyond my comprehension, he would
give me a little book to read; it was better
far, he maintained, to read, than to stare idly

MISS ISA BOWMAN AND MISS BESSIE HATTON AS THE
LITTLE PRINCES IN THE TOWER

about the church. When the rest of the con-
gregation rose at the entrance of the choir he
kept his seat. He argued that rising to one's
feet at such a time tended to make the choir-
boys conceited. I think he was quite right.

He kept no special books for Sunday reading, for he was most emphatically of opinion
that anything tending to make Sunday a day
dreaded by a child should be studiously avoided.
He did not like me to sew on Sunday unless
it was absolutely necessary.

One would hardly have expected that a
man of so reserved a nature as Lewis Carroll
would have taken much interest in the stage.
Yet he was devoted to the theatre, and one of
the commonest of the treats that he gave his
little girl friends was to organise a party for
the play. As a critic of acting he was naïve
and outspoken, and never hesitated to find
fault if he thought it justifiable. The following letter that he wrote to me criticising my
acting in " Richard III." when I was playing
with Richard Mansfield, is one of the most
interesting that I ever received from him.

ISA BOWMAN AS DUKE OF YORK

Although it was written for a child to understand and profit by, and moreover written in
the simplest possible way, it yet even now
strikes me as a trenchant and valuable piece
of criticism.

"Ch. Ch. Oxford,
Ap. 4, '89.

"My Lord Duke, — The photographs
which Your Grace did me the honour of sending arrived safely; and I can assure Your Royal
Highness that I am very glad to have them,
and like them *very* much, particularly the
large head of your late Royal Uncle's little
little son. I do not wonder that your excellent Uncle Richard should say 'off with
his head!' as a hint to the photographer to
print it off. Would your Highness like me
to go on calling you the Duke of York, or
shall I say 'my own own darling Isa?'
Which do you like best?

"Now I'm going to find fault with my pet
about her acting. What's the good of an
old Uncle like me except to find fault?

"You do the meeting with the Prince of

Wales *very* nicely and lovingly ; and, in teasing
your Uncle for his dagger and his sword,
you are very sweet and playful : and—'but
that's not finding fault !' Isa says to herself.
Isn't it ? Well, I'll try again. Didn't I hear
you say 'In weightier things you'll say a
beggar nay,' leaning on the word 'beggar' ?
If so, it was a mistake. *My* rule for knowing
which word to lean on is the word that tells
you something *new*, something that is *different*
from what you expected.

" Take the sentence 'first I bought a bag
of apples, then I bought a bag of pears,' you
wouldn't say 'then I bought a *bag* of pears.' The
' bag ' is nothing new, because it was a bag in
the first part of the sentence. But the *pears* are
new, and different from the *apples*. So you
would say, ' then I bought a bag of *pears*.'

" Do you understand that, my pet ?

" Now what you say to Richard amounts to
this, ' With light gifts you'll say to a beggar
" yes " : with heavy gifts you'll say to a
beggar " nay." ' The words ' you'll say to a
beggar, are the same both times ; so you

mustn't lean on any of *those* words. But
'light' is different from 'heavy,' and 'yes'
is different from 'nay.'   So the way to say
the sentence would be 'with *light* gifts you'll
say to a beggar "*yes*": with *heavy* gifts you'll
say to a beggar "*nay*".'   And the way to say
the lines in the play is—

> ' O, then I see you will *part* but with *light* gifts ;
> In *weightier* things you'll say a beggar *nay*.'

" One more sentence.

"When Richard says, 'What, would you
have my *weapon*, little Lord?' and you reply
'I *would*, that I might thank you as you call
me,' didn't I hear you pronounce 'thank' as
if it were spelt with an 'e'?   I know it's
very common (I often do it myself) to say
'thenk you!' as an exclamation by itself.   I
suppose it's an odd way of pronouncing the
word.   But I'm sure its wrong to pronounce
it so when it comes into a *sentence*.   It will
sound *much* nicer if you'll pronounce it so as
to rhyme with 'bank.'

"One more thing.   ('What an impertinent

old uncle! Always finding fault!') You're not as *natural*, when acting the Duke, as you were when you acted Alice. You seemed to me not to forgot *yourself* enough. It was not so much a real *prince* talking to his elder brother and his uncle; it was *Isa Bowman* talking to people she didn't *much* care about, for an audience to listen to—I don't mean it was that all *through*, but *sometimes* you were *artificial*. Now don't be jealous of Miss Hatton, when I say she was *sweetly* natural. She looked and spoke just like a *real* Prince of Wales. And she didn't seem to know that there was any audience. If you are ever to be a *good* actress (as I hope you will), you must learn to *forget* 'Isa' altogether, and *be* the character you are playing. Try to think 'This is *really* the Prince of Wales, I'm his little brother, and I'm *very* glad to meet him, and I love him *very* much,' and 'this is *really* my uncle: he's very kind, and lets me say saucy things to him,' and *do* forget that there's anybody else listening!

"My sweet pet, I *hope* you won't be offended

with me for saying what I fancy might make
your acting better !

            " Your loving old Uncle,
                        " CHARLES.

    × for NELLIE.
    × for MAGGIE.   × for ISA."
    × for EMSIE.

He was a fairly constant patron of all the
London theatres, save the Gaiety and the
Adelphi, which he did not like, and numbered
a good many theatrical folk among his ac-
quaintances.   Miss Ellen Terry was one of
his greatest friends.   Once I remember we
made an expedition from Eastbourne to Margate to visit Miss Sarah Thorne's theatre, and
especially for the purpose of seeing Miss
Violet Vanbrugh's Ophelia.   He was a great
admirer of both Miss Violet and Miss Irene
Vanbrugh as actresses.   Of Miss Thorne's
school of acting too he had the highest
opinion, and it was his often expressed wish
that all intending players could have so excellent a course of tuition.   Among the male
members of the theatrical profession he had

Miss Isa Bowman
as Alice in "Alice in "Wonderland."

no especial favourites, excepting Mr. Toole
and Mr. Richard Mansfield.

He never went to a music-hall, but considered that, properly managed, they might
be beneficial to the public. It was only when
the refrain of some particularly vulgar music-
hall song broke upon his ears in the streets,
that he permitted himself to speak harshly
about variety theatres.

Comic opera, when it was wholesome, he
liked, and was a frequent visitor to the Savoy
theatre. The good old style of Pantomime
too was a great delight to him, and he would
often speak affectionately of the pantomimes
at Brighton during the régime of Mr. and
Mrs. Nye Chart. But of the up-to-date
pantomime he had a horror, and nothing would
induce him to visit one. " When pantomimes
are written for children once more," he said,
" I will go. Not till then."

Once when a friend told him that she was
about to take her little girls to the pantomime,
he did not rest till he had dissuaded her.

To conclude what I have said about Lewis

Carroll's affection for the dramatic art, I will give a kind of examination paper, written for a child who had been learning a recitation called "The Demon of the Pit." Though his stuttering prevented him from being himself anything of a reciter, he loved correct elocution, and would take any pains to make a·child perfect in a piece.

First of all there is an explanatory paragraph.

"As you don't ask any questions about 'The Demon of the Pit,' I suppose you understand it all. So please answer these questions just as you would do if a younger child (say Mollie) asked them."

Mollie. Please, Ethel, will you explain this poem to me. There are some very hard words in it.

Ethel. What are they, dear?

Mollie. Well, in the first line, "If you chance to make a sally," what does "sally" mean?

Ethel. Dear Mollie, I believe sally means to take a chance work.[1]

[1] At this point the real child's answers begin, the three or four lines alone were written by Mr. Dodgson himself. — ED.

THE LITTLE PRINCES

Mollie. Then, near the end of the first verse —"Whereupon she'll call her cronies"—what does "whereupon" mean? And what are cronies?

Ethel. I think whereupon means at the same time, and cronies means her favourite play-fellows.

Mollie. "And invest in proud polonies." What's to "invest"?

Ethel. To invest means to spend money in anything you fancy.

Mollie. And what's "A woman of the day"?

Ethel. A woman of the day means a wonder of the time with the general public.

Mollie. "Pyrotechnic blaze of wit." What's pyrotechnic?

Ethel. Mollie, I think you will find that pyrotechnic means quick, with flashes of lightning.

Mollie. Then the 8 lines that begin "The astounding infant wonder"—please explain "rôle" and "mise" and "tout ensemble" and "grit."

Ethel. Well, Mollie, "rôle" means so many

different things, but in "The Demon of the
Pit" I should think it meant the leading part
of the piece, and "mise" means something extra
good introduced, and "tout" means to seek for
applause, but "ensemble" means the whole of
the parts taken together, and grit means
something good.

Mollie. "And the Goblins prostrate tumble,"
what's "prostrate"?

Ethel. I believe prostrate means to be cast
down and unhappy.

Mollie. "And his accents shake a bit."
What are "accents"?

Ethel. To accent is to lay stress upon a
word.

Mollie. "Waits resignedly behind." What's
"resignedly"?

Ethel. Resignedly means giving up, yield-
ing.

Mollie. "They have tripe as light to dream
on." What does "as" mean here? and what
does "to dream on" mean?

Ethel. Mollie dear, your last question is
very funny. In the first place, I have always

been told that hot suppers are not good for any one, and I should think that TRIPE would *not be light* to dream on but VERY heavy.

Mollie. Thank you, Ethel.

I have now nearly finished my little memoir of Lewis Carroll; that is to say, I have written down all that I can remember of my personal knowledge of him. But I think it is from the letters and the diaries published in this book that my readers must chiefly gain an insight into the character of the greatest friend to children who ever lived. Not only did he study children's ways for his own pleasure, but he studied them in order that he might please them. For instance, here is a letter that he wrote to my little sister Nelly eight years ago, which begins on the last page and is written entirely backwards—a kind of variant on his famous "Looking - Glass" writing. You have to begin at the last word and read backwards before you can understand it. The only ordinary thing about it is the date. It begins—I mean *begins* if one was to read it in the ordinary way, with the characteristic monogram, C. L. D.

"Nov. 1, 1891.

"C. L. D., Uncle loving your! Instead grandson his to it give to had you that so, years 80 or 70 for it forgot you that was it pity a what and : him of fond so were you wonder don't I and, gentleman old nice very a was he. For it made you that *him* been have *must* it see you so : *grandfather* my was, *then* alive was that, ' Dodgson Uncle ' only the. Born was *I* before long was that, see you, then But. ' Dodgson Uncle for pretty thing some make I'll now,' it began you when, yourself to said you that, me telling her without, knew I course of and : ago years many great a it made had you said she. Me told Isa what from was it ? For meant was it who out made I how know you do ! Lasted has it well how and. Grandfather my for made had you Antimacassar pretty that me give to you of nice so was it, Nelly dear my."

Nov. 1. 1891.

D, Uncle loving
your! Instead grand
-son his to it give to
had you that so, years
80 or 70 for it forgot
you that was it pity,
a what and : him of fond
So were you wonder don't
I and, gentleman old
nice very a was he. For
it made you that <u>him</u>
been have <u>must</u> it see
you so: grand<u>father</u> my
was, <u>then</u> alive was that,
"Dodgson Uncle" only
the. Born was <u>I</u> before

long was that, see you,
then But. "Dodgson
Uncle for pretty thing
some make I'll now",
it began you when,
yourself to said you
that, me telling her
without, know I course
of and : ago years many
great a it made had
you said she. Me told
I's a what from was it?
For meant was it who
out made I how know

*you do ! Lasted has it
well how and Grandfather
my for made had you
Antimacassar pretty
that me give to you of
nice so was it, Nelly
dear my.*

Miss Hatch has also sent me an original
letter that Lewis Carroll wrote to her in 1873,
about a large wax doll that he had given her.
It is interesting to notice that this letter, written
long before any of the others that he wrote to
me, is identically the same in form and expression. It is a striking proof how fresh and
unimpaired the writer's sympathies must have
been. Year after year he retained the same
sweet, kindly temperament, and, if anything, his
love for children seemed to increase as he
grew older.

"My dear Birdie,—I met her just outside Tom Gate, walking very stiffly, and I think she was trying to find her way to my rooms. So I said, 'Why have you come here without Birdie?' So she said, 'Birdie's gone! and Emily's gone! and Mabel isn't kind to me!' And two little waxy tears came running down her cheeks.

"Why, how stupid of me! I've never told you who it was all the time! It was your new doll. I was very glad to see her, and I took her to my room, and gave her some vesta matches to eat, and a cup of nice melted wax to drink, for the poor little thing was *very* hungry and thirsty after her long walk. So I said, 'Come and sit down by the fire, and let's have a comfortable chat?' 'Oh no! no!' she said, 'I'd *much* rather not. You know I do melt so *very* easily!' And she made me take her quite to the other side of the room, where it was *very* cold : and then she sat on my knee, and fanned herself with a pen-wiper, because she said she was afraid the end of her nose was beginning to melt.

"DOLLY VARDEN"

" ' You've no *idea* how careful we have to be, we dolls,' she said. ' Why, there was a sister of mine—would you believe it?—she went up to the fire to warm her hands, and one of her hands dropped *right* off! There now!' ' Of course it dropped *right* off,' I said, ' because it was the *right* hand.' ' And how do you know it was the *right* hand, Mister Carroll?' the doll said. So I said, ' I think it must have been the *right* hand because the other hand was *left*.'

" The doll said, ' I shan't laugh. It's a very bad joke. Why, even a common wooden doll could make a better joke than that. And besides, they've made my mouth so stiff and hard, that I *can't* laugh if I try ever so much?' ' Don't be cross about it,' I said, ' but tell me this : I'm going to give Birdie and the other children one photograph each, whichever they choose; which do you think Birdie will choose?' ' I don't know,' said the doll; ' you'd better ask her!' So I took her home in a hansom cab. Which would you like, do you think? Arthur as Cupid? or Arthur and Wilfred

together ? or you and Ethel as beggar children ?
or Ethel standing on a box ? or, one of yourself ?—Your affectionate friend,

                        " LEWIS CARROLL."

Among the bundle of letters and MS. before
me, I find written on a half sheet of note-
paper the following Ollendorfian dialogue.   It
is interesting because, slight and trivial as it is,
it in some strange way bears the imprint of
Lewis Carroll's style.   The thing is written in
the familiar violet ink, and neatly dated in the
corner 29/9/90 :—

"Let's go and look at the house I want
to buy.   Now do be quick !   You move so
slow !   What a time you take with your
boots ! "

"Don't make such a row about it : it's not
two o'clock yet.   How do you like *this*
house ? "

"I don't like it.   It's too far down the
hill.   Let's go higher.   I heard a nice account
of one at the top, built on an improved plan."

"What does the rent amount to?"

"Oh, the rent's all right: it's only nine pounds a year."

Over all matters connected with letter writing, Lewis Carroll was accustomed to take great pains. All letters that he received that were of any interest or importance whatever he kept, putting them away in old biscuit tins, numbers of which he kept for the purpose.

In 1888 he published a little book which he called "Eight or Nine Wise Words about Letter Writing," and as this little book of mine is so full of letters, I think I can do no better than make a few extracts :—

"*Write Legibly.*—The average temper of the human race would be perceptibly sweeter if every one obeyed this rule! A great deal of the bad writing in the world comes simply from writing too quickly. Of course you reply, 'I do it to save time.' A very good object, no doubt; but what right have you to do it at your friend's expense? Isn't *his*

time as valuable as yours?   Years ago I used
to receive letters from a friend — and very
interesting letters too—written in one of the
most atrocious hands ever invented.   It generally took me about a *week* to read one of his
letters !   I used to carry it about in my
pocket, and take it out at leisure times, to
puzzle over the riddles which composed it—
holding it in different positions, and at
different distances, till at last the meaning
of some hopeless scrawl would flash upon
me, when I at once wrote down the English
under it; and, when several had thus been
guessed, the context would help one with
the others, till at last the whole series of
hieroglyphics was deciphered.   If *all* one's
friends wrote like that, life would be entirely
spent in reading their letters."

In writing the last wise word, the author
no doubt had some of his girl correspondents
in his mind's eye, for he says—

" *My Ninth Rule.*—When you get to the
end of a note sheet, and find you have more

to say, take another piece of paper—a whole
sheet or a scrap, as the case may demand;
but, whatever you do, *don't cross!* Remember
the old proverb, 'Cross writing makes cross
reading.' 'The *old* proverb,' you say inquir-
ingly; 'how old?' Well, not so *very* ancient,
I must confess. In fact I'm afraid I invented
it while writing this paragraph. Still you
know 'old' is a comparative term. I think
you would be *quite* justified in addressing a
chicken just out of the shell as 'Old Boy!'
when compared with another chicken that was
only half out!'"

I have another diary to give to my readers,
a diary that Lewis Carroll wrote for my sister
Maggie when, a tiny child, she came to
Oxford to play the child part, Mignon, in
" Bootles' Baby." He was delighted with the
pretty play, for the interest that the soldiers
took in the little lost girl, and how a mere
interest ripened into love, till the little Mignon
was queen of the barracks, went straight to
his heart. I give the diary in full :—

"MAGGIE'S VISIT TO OXFORD

JUNE 9 TO 13, 1889

When Maggie once to Oxford came
    On tour as ' Bootles' Baby,'
She said ' I'll see this place of fame,
    However dull the day be ! '

So with her friend she visited
    The sights that it was rich in :
And first of all she poked her head
    Inside the Christ Church Kitchen.

The cooks around that little child
    Stood waiting in a ring :
And, every time that Maggie smiled,
    Those cooks began to sing—
    Shouting the Battle-cry of Freedom !

        ' Roast, boil, and bake,
        For Maggie's sake !
        Bring cutlets fine,
        For *her* to dine :
        Meringues so sweet,
        For *her* to eat—
        For Maggie may be
        Bootles' Baby ! '

Then hand-in-hand, in pleasant talk,
    They wandered, and admired
The Hall, Cathedral, and Broad Walk,
    Till Maggie's feet were tired :

One friend they called upon—her name
    Was Mrs. Hassall—then
Into a College Room they came,
    Some savage Monster's Den !

' And, when that Monster dined, I guess
    He tore her limb from limb ? '
Well, no : in fact, I must confess
    That *Maggie dined with him !*

To Worcester Garden next they strolled—
    Admired its quiet lake :
Then to St. John's, a College old,
    Their devious way they take.

In idle mood they sauntered round
    Its lawns so green and flat :
And in that Garden Maggie found
    A lovely Pussy-Cat !

A quarter of an hour they spent
    In wandering to and fro :
And everywhere that Maggie went,
    That Cat was sure to go—
    Shouting the Battle-cry of Freedom !

'Miaow! Miaow!
Come, make your bow!
Take off your hats,
Ye Pussy Cats!
And purr, and purr,
To welcome *her*—
For Maggie may be
Bootles' Baby!'

So back to Christ Church—not too late
    For them to go and see
A Christ Church Undergraduate,
    Who gave them cakes and tea.

Next day she entered, with her guide,
    The Garden called 'Botanic':
And there a fierce Wild-Boar she spied,
    Enough to cause a panic!

But Maggie didn't mind, not she!
    She would have faced *alone*,
That fierce Wild-Boar, because, you see,
    The thing was made of stone!

On Magdalen walls they saw a face
    That filled her with delight,
A giant-face, that made grimace
    And grinned with all its might!

A little friend, industrious,
    Pulled upwards, all the while,
The corner of its mouth, and thus
    He helped that face to smile!

'How nice,' thought Maggie, 'it would be
  If *I* could have a friend
To do that very thing for *me*,
And make my mouth turn up with glee,
  By pulling at one end!'

In Magdalen Park the deer are wild
  With joy that Maggie brings
Some bread a friend had given the child,
  To feed the pretty things.

They flock round Maggie without fear:
  They breakfast and they lunch,
They dine, they sup, those happy deer—
  Still, as they munch and munch,
  Shouting the Battle-cry of Freedom!

      'Yes, Deer are we,
      And dear is she!
      We love this child
      So sweet and mild:
      We all rejoice
      At Maggie's voice:
      We all are fed
      With Maggie's bread—
      For Maggie may be
      Bootles' Baby!'

To Pembroke College next they go,
  Where little Maggie meets
The Master's wife and daughter: so
  Once more into the streets.

They met a Bishop on their way—
A Bishop large as life—
With loving smile that seemed to say
'Will Maggie be my wife?'

Maggie thought *not*, because, you see,
She was so *very* young,
And he was old as old could be—
So Maggie held her tongue.

'My Lord, she's *Bootles' Baby* : we
Are going up and down,'
Her friend explained, 'that she may see
The sights of Oxford-town.'

'Now say what kind of place it is !'
The Bishop gaily cried.
'The best place in the Provinces !'
That little maid replied.

Next to New College, where they saw
Two players hurl about
A hoop, but by what rule or law
They could not quite make out.

'Ringo' the Game is called, although
'Les Graces' was once its name,
When *it* was—as its name will show—
A much more *graceful* Game.

The Misses Symonds next they sought,
    Who begged the child to take
A book they long ago had bought—
    A gift for friendship's sake !

Away, next morning, Maggie went
    From Oxford-town : but yet
The happy hours she there had spent
    She could not soon forget.

The train is gone : it rumbles on :
    The engine-whistle screams :
But Maggie's deep in rosy sleep—
    And softly, in her dreams,
      Whispers the Battle-cry of Freedom !

    ' Oxford, good-bye ! '
    She seems to sigh,
    ' You dear old City,
    With Gardens pretty,
    And lawns, and flowers,
    And College-towers,
    And Tom's great Bell—
    Farewell, farewell !
    For Maggie may be
    Bootles' Baby ! '
          —LEWIS CARROLL."

The tale has been often told of how " Alice in Wonderland " came to be written, but it is a tale so well worth the telling again, that, very shortly, I will give it to you here.

Years ago in the great quadrangle of Christ Church, opposite to Mr. Dodgson, lived the little daughters of Dean Liddell, the great Greek scholar and Dean of Christ Church. The little girls were great friends of Mr. Dodgson's, and they used often to come to him and to plead with him for a fairy tale. There was never such a teller of tales, they thought! One can imagine the whole delightful scene with little trouble. That big cool room on some summer's afternoon, when the air was heavy with flower scents, and the sounds that came floating in through the open window were all mellowed by the distance. One can see him, that good and kindly gentleman, his mobile face all aglow with interest and love, telling the immortal story.

Round him and on his knee sat the little sisters, their eyes wide open and their lips parted in breathless anticipation. When Alice (how the little Alice Liddell who was listening must have loved the tale!) rubbed the

"A TURK"

mushroom and became so big that she quite filled the little fairy house, one can almost hear the rapturous exclamations of the little ones as they heard of it.

The story, often continued on many summer afternoons, sometimes in the cool Christ Church rooms, sometimes in a slow gliding boat in a still river between banks of rushes and strange bronze and yellow waterflowers, or sometimes in a great hay-field, with the insects whispering in the grass all round, grew in its conception and idea.

Other folk, older folk, came to hear of it from the little ones, and Mr. Dodgson was begged to write it down. Accordingly the first MS. was prepared with great care and illustrated by the author. Then, in 1865, memorable year for English children, "Alice" appeared in its present form, with Sir John Tenniel's drawings.

In 1872 "Alice Through the Looking-Glass," appeared, and was received as warmly as its predecessor. That fact, I think, proves most conclusively that Lewis Carroll's success was a success of absolute merit, and due to no mere mood or fashion of the public taste. I can conceive nothing more difficult for a man who has had a great success with one book than to write a sequel which should worthily succeed it. In the present case that is exactly what Lewis Carroll did. "Through the Looking-Glass" is every whit as popular and charming as the older book. Indeed one depends very much upon the other, and in every child's book-shelves one sees the two masterpieces side by side.

A CHARADE.

[NB FIVE POUNDS will be
given to any one who succeeds in
writing an original poetical Cha-
-rade, introducing the line "My
First is followed by a bird," but
making no use of the answer to
this Charade   Ap 8 1878
          (signed)
            Lewis Carroll]

My First is singular at best
    More plural is my Second.
My Third is far the pluralest —
So plural-plural, I protest,
    It scarcely can be reckoned!

My First is followed by a bird
　　My Second by believers
In magic art · my simple Third
Follows, too often, hopes absurd,
　　And plausible deceivers.

My First to get at wisdom tries—
　　A failure melancholy!
My Second men revere as wise:
My Third from heights of wisdom fly
　　To depths of frantic folly!

My First is ageing day by day,
　　My Second's age is ended
My Third enjoys an age, they say,
That never seems to fade away,
　　Through centuries extended!

My Whole? I need a Poet's pen
    To paint her myriad phases
The monarch, and the slave, of men—
A mountain-summit, and a den
    Of dark and deadly mazes!

A flashing light— a fleeting shade—
    Beginning, end, and middle
Of all that human art hath made,
Or wit devised! Go, seek her aid,
    If you would guess my riddle!

While on the subject of the two " Alices," I will put in a letter that he wrote mentioning his books. He was so modest about them, that it was extremely difficult to get him to say, or write, anything at all about them. I believe it was a far greater pleasure for him to know that he had pleased some child with "Alice" or " The Hunting of the Snark," than it was to be hailed by the press and public as the first living writer for children.

" EASTBOURNE.

" MY OWN DARLING ISA,—The full value of a copy of the French ' Alice' is £45 : but, as you want the ' cheapest' kind, and as you are a great friend of mine, and as I am of a very noble, generous disposition, I have made up my mind to a *great* sacrifice, and have taken £3, 10s. 0d. off the price. So that you do not owe me more than £41, 10s. 0d., and this you can pay me, in gold or bank-notes, *as soon as you ever like*. Oh dear ! I wonder why I write such nonsense ! Can you explain to me, my pet, how it happens that when I take up my pen to write a letter to *you* it won't write

sense? Do you think the rule is that when
the pen finds it has to write to a nonsensical
good-for-nothing child, it sets to work to
write a nonsensical good-for-nothing letter?
Well, now I'll tell you the real truth. As
Miss Kitty Wilson is a dear friend of yours,
of course she's a *sort* of a friend of mine. So
I thought (in my vanity) 'perhaps she would
like to have a copy' from the author, 'with
her name written in it.' So I've sent her one
—but I hope she'll understand that I do it
because she's *your* friend, for, you see, I had
never *heard* of her before: so I wouldn't have
any other reason.

"I'm still exactly 'on the balance' (like
those scales of mine, when Nellie says 'it
won't weigh!') as to whether it would be
wise to have my pet Isa down here! how *am*
I to make it weigh, I wonder? Can you
advise any way to do it? I'm getting on
grandly with 'Sylvie and Bruno Concluded.'
I'm afraid you'll expect me to give you a copy
of it? Well, I'll see if I have one to spare.
It won't be out before Easter-tide, I'm afraid.

" I wonder what sort of condition the book is in that I lent you to take to America? ('Laneton Parsonage,' I mean). Very shabby, I expect. I find lent books *never* come back in good condition. However, I've got a second copy of this book, so you may keep it as your own. Love and kisses to any one you know who is lovely and kissable.—

   " Always your loving Uncle,
                              "C. L. D."

In 1876 appeared the long poem called the " Hunting of the Snark ; or, An Agony in Eight Fits," and besides those verses we have from Lewis Carroll's pen two books called " Phantasmagoria " and " Rhyme and Reason."

The last work of his that attained any great celebrity was " Sylvie and Bruno," a curious romance, half fairy tale, half mathematical treatise. Mr. Dodgson was employed of late years on his " Symbolic Logic," only one part of which has been published, and he seems to have been influenced by his studies. One can easily trace the trail of the logician in "Sylvie and Bruno," and perhaps this resulted in a certain lack of "form." However, some of the nonsense - verses in this book were up to the highest level of the author's achievement. Even as I write the verse comes to me—

> " He thought he saw a kangaroo
>   Turning a coffee-mill ;
> He looked again, and found it was
>   A vegetable pill !
> 'Were I to swallow you,' he said,
>   ' I should be very ill ' ! "

The fascinating jingle stays in the memory when graver verse eludes all effort at recollection. I personally could repeat "The Walrus and the Carpenter" from beginning to end without hesitation, but I should find a difficulty in writing ten lines of "Hamlet" correctly.

At the beginning of "Sylvie and Bruno" is a little poem in three verses which forms an acrostic on my name. I quote it—

> " Is all our life, then, but a dream,
>   Seen faintly in the golden gleam
>   Athwart Time's dark resistless stream ?

Bowed to the earth with bitter woe,
Or laughing at some raree-show,
We flutter idly to and fro.

Man's little day in haste we spend,
And, from it's merry noontide, send
No glance to meet the silent end."

You see that if you take the first letter of each line, or if you take the first three letters of the first line of each verse, you get the name Isa Bowman.

Although he never wrote anything in the dramatic line, he once wrote a prologue for some private theatricals, which was to be spoken by Miss Hatch and her brother. This prologue is reproduced in facsimile on the next page.

Miss Hatch has also sent me a charade (reproduced on pp. 114–116) which he wrote for her, and illustrated with some of his funny drawings.

I have another letter, which, as it mentions the book "Sylvie and Bruno," I will give now.

Prologue.

[Enter Beatrice, leading Wilfred. She leaves him
at centre (front), & after going round on tip-toe to
make sure they are not overheard returns & takes his arm]

B. "Wiffie! I'm sure that something is the matter!
All day there's been —— oh, such a fuss and clatter.
Mamma's been trying on a funny dress——
I never saw the house in such a mess!
        (puts her arm round his neck)
Is there a secret, Wiffie?"
                W. (shaking her off) "Yes, of course!"

B. " And you won't tell it? (whispers) Then you're very cross!
        (turns away from, & clasps her hands, looking up
                                                    ecstatically)
I'm sure of this! It's something quite uncommon!"
W. (stretching up his arms, with a mock-heroic air)
" Oh, Curiosity! Thy name is Woman!
        (puts his arm round her coaxingly)
Well, Birdie, then I'll 'tell' (mysteriously) What should you
                                                            say
If they were going to act —— a little play?"
B. (jumping and clapping her hands)
" I'd say 'How nice!' "
                W. (pointing to audience)
                "But will it please the rest?"
B. "Oh yes! Because, you know, they'll do their best!
        [turns to audience]
" You'll praise them, won't you, when you've seen the play?
Just say 'How nice!' before you go away!'"
        [they run away hand in hand].
                                        Feb 14. 1873.

"Christ Church,
"*May* 16, '90.

"Dearest Isa,—I had this ('this' was 'Sylvie and Bruno') bound for you when the book first came out, and it's been waiting here ever since Dec. 17, for I really didn't dare to send it across the Atlantic—the whales are so inconsiderate. They'd have been sure to want to borrow it to show to the little whales, quite forgetting that the salt water would be sure to spoil it.

"Also, I've only been waiting for you to get back to send Emsie the 'Nursery Alice.' I give it to the youngest in a family generally; but I've given one to Maggie as well, because she travels about so much, and I thought she would like to have one to take with her. I hope Nellie's eyes won't get *quite* green with jealousy, at two (indeed *three !*) of her sisters getting presents, and nothing for her! I've nothing but my love to send her to-day: but she shall have *something some* day.—Ever your loving UNCLE CHARLES."

Socially, Lewis Carroll was of strong con-
servative tendencies. He viewed with wonder
and a little pain the absolute levelling tendencies
of the last few years of his life. I have before
me an extremely interesting letter which deals
with social observances, and from which I am
able to make one or two extracts. The bulk
of the letter is of a private nature :—

"Ladies have 'to be *much*' more particular
than gentlemen in observing the distinctions
of what is called 'social position': and the
lower their own position is (in the scale of
'lady' ship), the more jealous they seem to
be in guarding it. . . . I've met with just the
same thing myself from people several degrees
above me. Not long ago I was staying in a
house along with a young lady (about twenty
years old, I should think) with a title of her
own, as she was an earl's daughter. I happened
to sit next her at dinner, and every time
I spoke to her, she looked at me more as
if she was looking down on me from about
a mile up in the air, and as if she were

saying to herself 'How *dare* you speak to *me*! Why, you're not good enough to black my shoes!' It was so unpleasant, that, next day at luncheon, I got as far off her as I could!

"Of course we are all *quite* equal in God's sight, but we *do* make a lot of distinctions (some of them quite unmeaning) among ourselves!"

The picture that this letter gives of the famous writer and learned mathematician obviously rather in terror of some pert young lady fresh from the schoolroom is not without its comic side. One cannot help imagining that the girl must have been very young indeed, for if he were alive to-day there are few ladies of any state who would not feel honoured by the presence of Charles Dodgson.

However, he was not always so unfortunate in his experience of great people, and the following letter, written when he was staying with Lord Salisbury at Hatfield House, tells delightfully of his little royal friends, the Duchess of Albany's children :—

June 8/89

My darling Isa,

I hope this will find
you, but I haven't yet
had any letter, written
from Fulham, so I can't
be sure if you have yet
got into your new house.

This is Lord Salisbury's
house (he is the father, you
know, of that Lady Maud
Wolmer that we had luncheon
with): I came yesterday, &
I'm going to stay until

Monday. It is such a nice house to stay in! They let one do just as one likes —— it isn't "now you must do some geography! now it's time for your sums"! the sort of life *some* little girls have to lead when they are so foolish as to visit friends —— but one can just please one's own dear self. There are some sweet little children staying in the house. Dear little "Wang" is here, with her mother. By the way, I made a mistake in telling you what to call her.

She is 'the Honourable Mabel Palmer'. 'Palmer' is the family name: 'Wolmer' is the title. Just as the family name of Lord Salisbury is 'Cecil': so that his daughter was Lady Maud Cecil, till she married.

Then there is the Duchess of Albany here, with two such sweet little children. She is the widow of Prince Leopold (the Queen's youngest son), so her children are a Prince & Princess: the girl is 'Alice', but I don't know the boy's Christian name: they call him 'Albany', because he is the Duke of Albany. Now that

I have made
friends with a
real live little
Princess, I don't
intend ever to
<u>speak</u> to any more children
that haven't titles. In fact,
I'm so proud, & I hold my chin
so high, that I shouldn't even
<u>see</u> you if we met! No, darling
you mustn't believe <u>that</u>. If
I made friends with a <u>dozen</u>
Princesses, I would love you
better than all of them together,
even I had them all rolled up
into a sort of child-roly-poly.

Love to Nellie & Emsie.

Your ever loving Uncle
C.L.D.

* * * * * * *

"Hatfield House, Hatfield,
"Herts, *June* 8/89.

"My darling Isa,—I hope this will find
you, but I haven't yet had any letter, written
from *Fulham*, so I can't be sure if you have
yet got into your new house.

"This is Lord Salisbury's house (he is the
father, you know, of that Lady Maud Wolmer
that we had luncheon with): I came yesterday,
and I'm going to stay until Monday. It is
such a nice house to stay in! They let one do
just as one likes—it isn't 'Now you must do
some geography! now it's time for your
sums!' the sort of life *some* little girls have
to lead when they are so foolish as to visit
friends—but one can just please one's own
dear self.

"There are some sweet little children staying
in the house. Dear little 'Wang' is here
with her mother. By the way, *I* made a
mistake in telling you what to call her. She
is 'the Honourable Mabel *Palmer*'—'Palmer'
is the *family* name: 'Wolmer' is the *title*, just

as the family name of Lord Salisbury is 'Cecil,' so that his daughter was Lady Maud Cecil, till she married.

"Then there is the Duchess of Albany here, with two such sweet little children. She is the widow of Prince Leopold (the Queen's youngest son), so her children are a Prince and Princess : the girl is 'Alice,' but I don't know the boy's Christian name : they call him 'Albany,' because he is the Duke of Albany. Now that I have made friends with a real live little Princess, I don't intend ever to *speak* to any more children that haven't any titles. In fact, I'm so proud, and I hold my chin so high, that I shouldn't even *see* you if we met ! No, darling, you mustn't believe *that*. If I made friends with a *dozen* Princesses, I would love you better than all of them together, even if I had them all rolled up into a sort of child-roly-poly.

"Love to Nellie and Emsie.—Your ever loving Uncle,   C. L. D."

And now I think that I have done all that has been in my power to present Lewis Carroll to you in his most delightful aspect—as a friend to children. I have not pretended in any way to write an exhaustive life-story of the man who was so dear to me, but by the aid of the letters and the diaries that I have been enabled to publish, and by the few reminiscences that I have given you of Lewis Carroll as I knew him, I hope I have done something to bring still nearer to your hearts the memory of the greatest friend that children ever had.

THE END

A CATALOGUE OF SELECTED DOVER BOOKS
IN ALL FIELDS OF INTEREST

AMERICA'S OLD MASTERS, James T. Flexner. Four men emerged unexpectedly from provincial 18th century America to leadership in European art: Benjamin West, J. S. Copley, C. R. Peale, Gilbert Stuart. Brilliant coverage of lives and contributions. Revised, 1967 edition. 69 plates. 365pp. of text.
21806-6 Paperbound $3.00

FIRST FLOWERS OF OUR WILDERNESS: AMERICAN PAINTING, THE COLONIAL PERIOD, James T. Flexner. Painters, and regional painting traditions from earliest Colonial times up to the emergence of Copley, West and Peale Sr., Foster, Gustavus Hesselius, Feke, John Smibert and many anonymous painters in the primitive manner. Engaging presentation, with 162 illustrations. xxii + 368pp.
22180-6 Paperbound $3.50

THE LIGHT OF DISTANT SKIES: AMERICAN PAINTING, 1760-1835, James T. Flexner. The great generation of early American painters goes to Europe to learn and to teach: West, Copley, Gilbert Stuart and others. Allston, Trumbull, Morse; also contemporary American painters—primitives, derivatives, academics—who remained in America. 102 illustrations. xiii + 306pp.
22179-2 Paperbound $3.00

A HISTORY OF THE RISE AND PROGRESS OF THE ARTS OF DESIGN IN THE UNITED STATES, William Dunlap. Much the richest mine of information on early American painters, sculptors, architects, engravers, miniaturists, etc. The only source of information for scores of artists, the major primary source for many others. Unabridged reprint of rare original 1834 edition, with new introduction by James T. Flexner, and 394 new illustrations. Edited by Rita Weiss. 6⅝ x 9⅝.
21695-0, 21696-9, 21697-7 Three volumes, Paperbound $13.50

EPOCHS OF CHINESE AND JAPANESE ART, Ernest F. Fenollosa. From primitive Chinese art to the 20th century, thorough history, explanation of every important art period and form, including Japanese woodcuts; main stress on China and Japan, but Tibet, Korea also included. Still unexcelled for its detailed, rich coverage of cultural background, aesthetic elements, diffusion studies, particularly of the historical period. 2nd, 1913 edition. 242 illustrations. lii + 439pp. of text.
20364-6, 20365-4 Two volumes, Paperbound $6.00

THE GENTLE ART OF MAKING ENEMIES, James A. M. Whistler. Greatest wit of his day deflates Oscar Wilde, Ruskin, Swinburne; strikes back at inane critics, exhibitions, art journalism; aesthetics of impressionist revolution in most striking form. Highly readable classic by great painter. Reproduction of edition designed by Whistler. Introduction by Alfred Werner. xxxvi + 334pp.
21875-9 Paperbound $2.50

A CATALOGUE OF SELECTED DOVER BOOKS
IN ALL FIELDS OF INTEREST

VISUAL ILLUSIONS: THEIR CAUSES, CHARACTERISTICS, AND APPLICATIONS, Matthew Luckiesh. Thorough description and discussion of optical illusion, geometric and perspective, particularly; size and shape distortions, illusions of color, of motion; natural illusions; use of illusion in art and magic, industry, etc. Most useful today with op art, also for classical art. Scores of effects illustrated. Introduction by William H. Ittleson. 100 illustrations. xxi + 252pp.

21530-X Paperbound $2.00

A HANDBOOK OF ANATOMY FOR ART STUDENTS, Arthur Thomson. Thorough, virtually exhaustive coverage of skeletal structure, musculature, etc. Full text, supplemented by anatomical diagrams and drawings and by photographs of undraped figures. Unique in its comparison of male and female forms, pointing out differences of contour, texture, form. 211 figures, 40 drawings, 86 photographs. xx + 459pp. 5⅜ x 8⅜.

21163-0 Paperbound $3.50

150 MASTERPIECES OF DRAWING, Selected by Anthony Toney. Full page reproductions of drawings from the early 16th to the end of the 18th century, all beautifully reproduced: Rembrandt, Michelangelo, Dürer, Fragonard, Urs, Graf, Wouwerman, many others. First-rate browsing book, model book for artists. xviii + 150pp. 8⅜ x 11¼.

21032-4 Paperbound $2.50

THE LATER WORK OF AUBREY BEARDSLEY, Aubrey Beardsley. Exotic, erotic, ironic masterpieces in full maturity: Comedy Ballet, Venus and Tannhauser, Pierrot, Lysistrata, Rape of the Lock, Savoy material, Ali Baba, Volpone, etc. This material revolutionized the art world, and is still powerful, fresh, brilliant. With *The Early Work,* all Beardsley's finest work. 174 plates, 2 in color. xiv + 176pp. 8⅛ x 11.

21817-1 Paperbound $3.00

DRAWINGS OF REMBRANDT, Rembrandt van Rijn. Complete reproduction of fabulously rare edition by Lippmann and Hofstede de Groot, completely reedited, updated, improved by Prof. Seymour Slive, Fogg Museum. Portraits, Biblical sketches, landscapes, Oriental types, nudes, episodes from classical mythology—All Rembrandt's fertile genius. Also selection of drawings by his pupils and followers. "Stunning volumes," *Saturday Review.* 550 illustrations. lxxviii + 552pp. 9⅛ x 12¼.

21485-0, 21486-9 Two volumes, Paperbound $7.00

THE DISASTERS OF WAR, Francisco Goya. One of the masterpieces of Western civilization—83 etchings that record Goya's shattering, bitter reaction to the Napoleonic war that swept through Spain after the insurrection of 1808 and to war in general. Reprint of the first edition, with three additional plates from Boston's Museum of Fine Arts. All plates facsimile size. Introduction by Philip Hofer, Fogg Museum. v + 97pp. 9⅜ x 8¼.

21872-4 Paperbound $2.00

GRAPHIC WORKS OF ODILON REDON. Largest collection of Redon's graphic works ever assembled: 172 lithographs, 28 etchings and engravings, 9 drawings. These include some of his most famous works. All the plates from *Odilon Redon: oeuvre graphique complet,* plus additional plates. New introduction and caption translations by Alfred Werner. 209 illustrations. xxvii + 209pp. 9⅛ x 12¼.

21966-8 Paperbound $4.00

DESIGN BY ACCIDENT; A BOOK OF "ACCIDENTAL EFFECTS" FOR ARTISTS AND DESIGNERS, James F. O'Brien. Create your own unique, striking, imaginative effects by "controlled accident" interaction of materials: paints and lacquers, oil and water based paints, splatter, crackling materials, shatter, similar items. Everything you do will be different; first book on this limitless art, so useful to both fine artist and commercial artist. Full instructions. 192 plates showing "accidents," 8 in color. viii + 215pp. 8⅜ x 11¼.　　　　　21942-9 Paperbound $3.50

THE BOOK OF SIGNS, Rudolf Koch. Famed German type designer draws 493 beautiful symbols: religious, mystical, alchemical, imperial, property marks, runes, etc. Remarkable fusion of traditional and modern. Good for suggestions of timelessness, smartness, modernity. Text. vi + 104pp. 6⅛ x 9¼.
　　　　　　　　　　　　　　　　20162-7 Paperbound $1.25

HISTORY OF INDIAN AND INDONESIAN ART, Ananda K. Coomaraswamy. An unabridged republication of one of the finest books by a great scholar in Eastern art. Rich in descriptive material, history, social backgrounds; Sunga reliefs, Rajput paintings, Gupta temples, Burmese frescoes, textiles, jewelry, sculpture, etc. 400 photos. viii + 423pp. 6⅜ x 9¾.　　　　　21436-2 Paperbound $4.00

PRIMITIVE ART, Franz Boas. America's foremost anthropologist surveys textiles, ceramics, woodcarving, basketry, metalwork, etc.; patterns, technology, creation of symbols, style origins. All areas of world, but very full on Northwest Coast Indians. More than 350 illustrations of baskets, boxes, totem poles, weapons, etc. 378 pp.
　　　　　　　　　　　　　　　　20025-6 Paperbound $3.00

THE GENTLEMAN AND CABINET MAKER'S DIRECTOR, Thomas Chippendale. Full reprint (third edition, 1762) of most influential furniture book of all time, by master cabinetmaker. 200 plates, illustrating chairs, sofas, mirrors, tables, cabinets, plus 24 photographs of surviving pieces. Biographical introduction by N. Bienenstock. vi + 249pp. 9⅞ x 12¾.　　　　　21601-2 Paperbound $4.00

AMERICAN ANTIQUE FURNITURE, Edgar G. Miller, Jr. The basic coverage of all American furniture before 1840. Individual chapters cover type of furniture— clocks, tables, sideboards, etc.—chronologically, with inexhaustible wealth of data. More than 2100 photographs, all identified, commented on. Essential to all early American collectors. Introduction by H. E. Keyes. vi + 1106pp. 7⅞ x 10¾.
　　　　　21599-7, 21600-4 Two volumes, Paperbound $11.00

PENNSYLVANIA DUTCH AMERICAN FOLK ART, Henry J. Kauffman. 279 photos, 28 drawings of tulipware, Fraktur script, painted tinware, toys, flowered furniture, quilts, samplers, hex signs, house interiors, etc. Full descriptive text. Excellent for tourist, rewarding for designer, collector. Map. 146pp. 7⅞ x 10¾.
　　　　　　　　　　　　　　　　21205-X Paperbound $2.50

EARLY NEW ENGLAND GRAVESTONE RUBBINGS, Edmund V. Gillon, Jr. 43 photographs, 226 carefully reproduced rubbings show heavily symbolic, sometimes macabre early gravestones, up to early 19th century. Remarkable early American primitive art, occasionally strikingly beautiful; always powerful. Text. xxvi + 207pp. 8⅜ x 11¼.　　　　　21380-3 Paperbound $3.50

ALPHABETS AND ORNAMENTS, Ernst Lehner. Well-known pictorial source for decorative alphabets, script examples, cartouches, frames, decorative title pages, calligraphic initials, borders, similar material. 14th to 19th century, mostly European. Useful in almost any graphic arts designing, varied styles. 750 illustrations. 256pp. 7 x 10. 21905-4 Paperbound $4.00

PAINTING: A CREATIVE APPROACH, Norman Colquhoun. For the beginner simple guide provides an instructive approach to painting: major stumbling blocks for beginner; overcoming them, technical points; paints and pigments; oil painting; watercolor and other media and color. New section on "plastic" paints. Glossary. Formerly *Paint Your Own Pictures.* 221pp. 22000-1 Paperbound $1.75

THE ENJOYMENT AND USE OF COLOR, Walter Sargent. Explanation of the relations between colors themselves and between colors in nature and art, including hundreds of little-known facts about color values, intensities, effects of high and low illumination, complementary colors. Many practical hints for painters, references to great masters. 7 color plates, 29 illustrations. x + 274pp. 20944-X Paperbound $2.75

THE NOTEBOOKS OF LEONARDO DA VINCI, compiled and edited by Jean Paul Richter. 1566 extracts from original manuscripts reveal the full range of Leonardo's versatile genius: all his writings on painting, sculpture, architecture, anatomy, astronomy, geography, topography, physiology, mining, music, etc., in both Italian and English, with 186 plates of manuscript pages and more than 500 additional drawings. Includes studies for the Last Supper, the lost Sforza monument, and other works. Total of xlvii + 866pp. 7⅞ x 10¾. 22572-0, 22573-9 Two volumes, Paperbound $10.00

MONTGOMERY WARD CATALOGUE OF 1895. Tea gowns, yards of flannel and pillow-case lace, stereoscopes, books of gospel hymns, the New Improved Singer Sewing Machine, side saddles, milk skimmers, straight-edged razors, high-button shoes, spittoons, and on and on . . . listing some 25,000 items, practically all illustrated. Essential to the shoppers of the 1890's, it is our truest record of the spirit of the period. Unaltered reprint of Issue No. 57, Spring and Summer 1895. Introduction by Boris Emmet. Innumerable illustrations. xiii + 624pp. 8½ x 11⅝. 22377-9 Paperbound $6.95

THE CRYSTAL PALACE EXHIBITION ILLUSTRATED CATALOGUE (LONDON, 1851). One of the wonders of the modern world—the Crystal Palace Exhibition in which all the nations of the civilized world exhibited their achievements in the arts and sciences—presented in an equally important illustrated catalogue. More than 1700 items pictured with accompanying text—ceramics, textiles, cast-iron work, carpets, pianos, sleds, razors, wall-papers, billiard tables, beehives, silverware and hundreds of other artifacts—represent the focal point of Victorian culture in the Western World. Probably the largest collection of Victorian decorative art ever assembled— indispensable for antiquarians and designers. Unabridged republication of the Art-Journal Catalogue of the Great Exhibition of 1851, with all terminal essays. New introduction by John Gloag, F.S.A. xxxiv + 426pp. 9 x 12. 22503-8 Paperbound $4.50

A History of Costume, Carl Köhler. Definitive history, based on surviving pieces of clothing primarily, and paintings, statues, etc. secondarily. Highly readable text, supplemented by 594 illustrations of costumes of the ancient Mediterranean peoples, Greece and Rome, the Teutonic prehistoric period; costumes of the Middle Ages, Renaissance, Baroque, 18th and 19th centuries. Clear, measured patterns are provided for many clothing articles. Approach is practical throughout. Enlarged by Emma von Sichart. 464pp.   21030-8 Paperbound $3.50

Oriental Rugs, Antique and Modern, Walter A. Hawley. A complete and authoritative treatise on the Oriental rug—where they are made, by whom and how, designs and symbols, characteristics in detail of the six major groups, how to distinguish them and how to buy them. Detailed technical data is provided on periods, weaves, warps, wefts, textures, sides, ends and knots, although no technical background is required for an understanding. 11 color plates, 80 halftones, 4 maps. vi + 320pp. 6⅛ x 9⅛.   22366-3 Paperbound $5.00

Ten Books on Architecture, Vitruvius. By any standards the most important book on architecture ever written. Early Roman discussion of aesthetics of building, construction methods, orders, sites, and every other aspect of architecture has inspired, instructed architecture for about 2,000 years. Stands behind Palladio, Michelangelo, Bramante, Wren, countless others. Definitive Morris H. Morgan translation. 68 illustrations. xii + 331pp.   20645-9 Paperbound $2.50

The Four Books of Architecture, Andrea Palladio. Translated into every major Western European language in the two centuries following its publication in 1570, this has been one of the most influential books in the history of architecture. Complete reprint of the 1738 Isaac Ware edition. New introduction by Adolf Placzek, Columbia Univ. 216 plates. xxii + 110pp. of text. 9½ x 12¾.
                                                      21308-0 Clothbound $10.00

Sticks and Stones: A Study of American Architecture and Civilization, Lewis Mumford.One of the great classics of American cultural history. American architecture from the medieval-inspired earliest forms to the early 20th century; evolution of structure and style, and reciprocal influences on environment. 21 photographic illustrations. 238pp.   20202-X Paperbound $2.00

The American Builder's Companion, Asher Benjamin. The most widely used early 19th century architectural style and source book, for colonial up into Greek Revival periods. Extensive development of geometry of carpentering, construction of sashes, frames, doors, stairs; plans and elevations of domestic and other buildings. Hundreds of thousands of houses were built according to this book, now invaluable to historians, architects, restorers, etc. 1827 edition. 59 plates. 114pp. 7⅞ x 10¾.
                                                      22236-5 Paperbound $3.00

Dutch Houses in the Hudson Valley Before 1776, Helen Wilkinson Reynolds. The standard survey of the Dutch colonial house and outbuildings, with constructional features, decoration, and local history associated with individual homesteads. Introduction by Franklin D. Roosevelt. Map. 150 illustrations. 469pp. 6⅝ x 9¼.   21469-9 Paperbound $4.00

THE ARCHITECTURE OF COUNTRY HOUSES, Andrew J. Downing. Together with Vaux's *Villas and Cottages* this is the basic book for Hudson River Gothic architecture of the middle Victorian period. Full, sound discussions of general aspects of housing, architecture, style, decoration, furnishing, together with scores of detailed house plans, illustrations of specific buildings, accompanied by full text. Perhaps the most influential single American architectural book. 1850 edition. Introduction by J. Stewart Johnson. 321 figures, 34 architectural designs. xvi + 560pp.
22003-6 Paperbound $4.00

LOST EXAMPLES OF COLONIAL ARCHITECTURE, John Mead Howells. Full-page photographs of buildings that have disappeared or been so altered as to be denatured, including many designed by major early American architects. 245 plates. xvii + 248pp. 7⅞ x 10¾. 21143-6 Paperbound $3.50

DOMESTIC ARCHITECTURE OF THE AMERICAN COLONIES AND OF THE EARLY REPUBLIC, Fiske Kimball. Foremost architect and restorer of Williamsburg and Monticello covers nearly 200 homes between 1620-1825. Architectural details, construction, style features, special fixtures, floor plans, etc. Generally considered finest work in its area. 219 illustrations of houses, doorways, windows, capital mantels. xx + 314pp. 7⅞ x 10¾. 21743-4 Paperbound $4.00

EARLY AMERICAN ROOMS: 1650-1858, edited by Russell Hawes Kettell. Tour of 12 rooms, each representative of a different era in American history and each furnished, decorated, designed and occupied in the style of the era. 72 plans and elevations, 8-page color section, etc., show fabrics, wall papers, arrangements, etc. Full descriptive text. xvii + 200pp. of text. 8⅜ x 11¼.
21633-0 Paperbound $5.00

THE FITZWILLIAM VIRGINAL BOOK, edited by J. Fuller Maitland and W. B. Squire. Full modern printing of famous early 17th-century ms. volume of 300 works by Morley, Byrd, Bull, Gibbons, etc. For piano or other modern keyboard instrument; easy to read format. xxxvi + 938pp. 8⅜ x 11.
21068-5, 21069-3 Two volumes, Paperbound $10.00

KEYBOARD MUSIC, Johann Sebastian Bach. Bach Gesellschaft edition. A rich selection of Bach's masterpieces for the harpsichord: the six English Suites, six French Suites, the six Partitas (Clavierübung part I), the Goldberg Variations (Clavierübung part IV), the fifteen Two-Part Inventions and the fifteen Three-Part Sinfonias. Clearly reproduced on large sheets with ample margins; eminently playable. vi + 312pp. 8⅛ x 11. 22360-4 Paperbound $5.00

THE MUSIC OF BACH: AN INTRODUCTION, Charles Sanford Terry. A fine, non-technical introduction to Bach's music, both instrumental and vocal. Covers organ music, chamber music, passion music, other types. Analyzes themes, developments, innovations. x + 114pp. 21075-8 Paperbound $1.25

BEETHOVEN AND HIS NINE SYMPHONIES, Sir George Grove. Noted British musicologist provides best history, analysis, commentary on symphonies. Very thorough, rigorously accurate; necessary to both advanced student and amateur music lover. 436 musical passages. vii + 407 pp. 20334-4 Paperbound $2.75

JOHANN SEBASTIAN BACH, Philipp Spitta. One of the great classics of musicology, this definitive analysis of Bach's music (and life) has never been surpassed. Lucid, nontechnical analyses of hundreds of pieces (30 pages devoted to St. Matthew Passion, 26 to B Minor Mass). Also includes major analysis of 18th-century music. 450 musical examples. 40-page musical supplement. Total of xx + 1799pp.

(EUK) 22278-0, 22279-9 Two volumes, Clothbound $17.50

MOZART AND HIS PIANO CONCERTOS, Cuthbert Girdlestone. The only full-length study of an important area of Mozart's creativity. Provides detailed analyses of all 23 concertos, traces inspirational sources. 417 musical examples. Second edition. 509pp.

(USO) 21271-8 Paperbound $3.50

THE PERFECT WAGNERITE: A COMMENTARY ON THE NIBLUNG'S RING, George Bernard Shaw. Brilliant and still relevant criticism in remarkable essays on Wagner's Ring cycle, Shaw's ideas on political and social ideology behind the plots, role of Leitmotifs, vocal requisites, etc. Prefaces. xxi + 136pp.

21707-8 Paperbound $1.50

DON GIOVANNI, W. A. Mozart. Complete libretto, modern English translation; biographies of composer and librettist; accounts of early performances and critical reaction. Lavishly illustrated. All the material you need to understand and appreciate this great work. Dover Opera Guide and Libretto Series; translated and introduced by Ellen Bleiler. 92 illustrations. 209pp.

21134-7 Paperbound $1.50

HIGH FIDELITY SYSTEMS: A LAYMAN'S GUIDE, Roy F. Allison. All the basic information you need for setting up your own audio system: high fidelity and stereo record players, tape records, F.M. Connections, adjusting tone arm, cartridge, checking needle alignment, positioning speakers, phasing speakers, adjusting hums, trouble-shooting, maintenance, and similar topics. Enlarged 1965 edition. More than 50 charts, diagrams, photos. iv + 91pp. 21514-8 Paperbound $1.25

REPRODUCTION OF SOUND, Edgar Villchur. Thorough coverage for laymen of high fidelity systems, reproducing systems in general, needles, amplifiers, preamps, loudspeakers, feedback, explaining physical background. "A rare talent for making technicalities vividly comprehensible," R. Darrell, *High Fidelity.* 69 figures. iv + 92pp. 21515-6 Paperbound $1.25

HEAR ME TALKIN' TO YA: THE STORY OF JAZZ AS TOLD BY THE MEN WHO MADE IT, Nat Shapiro and Nat Hentoff. Louis Armstrong, Fats Waller, Jo Jones, Clarence Williams, Billy Holiday, Duke Ellington, Jelly Roll Morton and dozens of other jazz greats tell how it was in Chicago's South Side, New Orleans, depression Harlem and the modern West Coast as jazz was born and grew. xvi + 429pp.

21726-4 Paperbound $2.50

FABLES OF AESOP, translated by Sir Roger L'Estrange. A reproduction of the very rare 1931 Paris edition; a selection of the most interesting fables, together with 50 imaginative drawings by Alexander Calder. v + 128pp. 6½x9¼.

21780-9 Paperbound $1.50

AGAINST THE GRAIN (A REBOURS), Joris K. Huysmans. Filled with weird images, evidences of a bizarre imagination, exotic experiments with hallucinatory drugs, rich tastes and smells and the diversions of its sybarite hero Duc Jean des Esseintes, this classic novel pushed 19th-century literary decadence to its limits. Full unabridged edition. Do not confuse this with abridged editions generally sold. Introduction by Havelock Ellis. xlix + 206pp.   22190-3 Paperbound $2.00

VARIORUM SHAKESPEARE: HAMLET. Edited by Horace H. Furness; a landmark of American scholarship. Exhaustive footnotes and appendices treat all doubtful words and phrases, as well as suggested critical emendations throughout the play's history. First volume contains editor's own text, collated with all Quartos and Folios. Second volume contains full first Quarto, translations of Shakespeare's sources (Belleforest, and Saxo Grammaticus), Der Bestrafte Brudermord, and many essays on critical and historical points of interest by major authorities of past and present. Includes details of staging and costuming over the years. By far the best edition available for serious students of Shakespeare. Total of xx + 905pp.
21004-9, 21005-7, 2 volumes, Paperbound $7.00

A LIFE OF WILLIAM SHAKESPEARE, Sir Sidney Lee. This is the standard life of Shakespeare, summarizing everything known about Shakespeare and his plays. Incredibly rich in material, broad in coverage, clear and judicious, it has served thousands as the best introduction to Shakespeare. 1931 edition. 9 plates. xxix + 792pp.   (USO) 21967-4 Paperbound $3.75

MASTERS OF THE DRAMA, John Gassner. Most comprehensive history of the drama in print, covering every tradition from Greeks to modern Europe and America, including India, Far East, etc. Covers more than 800 dramatists, 2000 plays, with biographical material, plot summaries, theatre history, criticism, etc. "Best of its kind in English," *New Republic*. 77 illustrations. xxii + 890pp.
20100-7 Clothbound $8.50

THE EVOLUTION OF THE ENGLISH LANGUAGE, George McKnight. The growth of English, from the 14th century to the present. Unusual, non-technical account presents basic information in very interesting form: sound shifts, change in grammar and syntax, vocabulary growth, similar topics. Abundantly illustrated with quotations. Formerly *Modern English in the Making*. xii + 590pp.
21932-1 Paperbound $3.50

AN ETYMOLOGICAL DICTIONARY OF MODERN ENGLISH, Ernest Weekley. Fullest, richest work of its sort, by foremost British lexicographer. Detailed word histories, including many colloquial and archaic words; extensive quotations. Do not confuse this with the Concise Etymological Dictionary, which is much abridged. Total of xxvii + 830pp. 6½ x 9¼.
21873-2, 21874-0 Two volumes, Paperbound $6.00

FLATLAND: A ROMANCE OF MANY DIMENSIONS, E. A. Abbott. Classic of science-fiction explores ramifications of life in a two-dimensional world, and what happens when a three-dimensional being intrudes. Amusing reading, but also useful as introduction to thought about hyperspace. Introduction by Banesh Hoffmann. 16 illustrations. xx + 103pp.   20001-9 Paperbound $1.00

POEMS OF ANNE BRADSTREET, edited with an introduction by Robert Hutchinson. A new selection of poems by America's first poet and perhaps the first significant woman poet in the English language. 48 poems display her development in works of considerable variety—love poems, domestic poems, religious meditations, formal elegies, "quaternions," etc. Notes, bibliography. viii + 222pp.
22160-1 Paperbound $2.00

THREE GOTHIC NOVELS: THE CASTLE OF OTRANTO BY HORACE WALPOLE; VATHEK BY WILLIAM BECKFORD; THE VAMPYRE BY JOHN POLIDORI, WITH FRAGMENT OF A NOVEL BY LORD BYRON, edited by E. F. Bleiler. The first Gothic novel, by Walpole; the finest Oriental tale in English, by Beckford; powerful Romantic supernatural story in versions by Polidori and Byron. All extremely important in history of literature; all still exciting, packed with supernatural thrills, ghosts, haunted castles, magic, etc. xl + 291pp.
21232-7 Paperbound $2.00

THE BEST TALES OF HOFFMANN, E. T. A. Hoffmann. 10 of Hoffmann's most important stories, in modern re-editings of standard translations: Nutcracker and the King of Mice, Signor Formica, Automata, The Sandman, Rath Krespel, The Golden Flowerpot, Master Martin the Cooper, The Mines of Falun, The King's Betrothed, A New Year's Eve Adventure. 7 illustrations by Hoffmann. Edited by E. F. Bleiler. xxxix + 419pp.
21793-0 Paperbound $2.50

GHOST AND HORROR STORIES OF AMBROSE BIERCE, Ambrose Bierce. 23 strikingly modern stories of the horrors latent in the human mind: The Eyes of the Panther, The Damned Thing, An Occurrence at Owl Creek Bridge, An Inhabitant of Carcosa, etc., plus the dream-essay, Visions of the Night. Edited by E. F. Bleiler. xxii + 199pp.
20767-6 Paperbound $1.50

BEST GHOST STORIES OF J. S. LeFANU, J. Sheridan LeFanu. Finest stories by Victorian master often considered greatest supernatural writer of all. Carmilla, Green Tea, The Haunted Baronet, The Familiar, and 12 others. Most never before available in the U. S. A. Edited by E. F. Bleiler. 8 illustrations from Victorian publications. xvii + 467pp.
20415-4 Paperbound $3.00

THE TIME STREAM, THE GREATEST ADVENTURE, AND THE PURPLE SAPPHIRE— THREE SCIENCE FICTION NOVELS, John Taine (Eric Temple Bell). Great American mathematician was also foremost science fiction novelist of the 1920's. *The Time Stream,* one of all-time classics, uses concepts of circular time; *The Greatest Adventure,* incredibly ancient biological experiments from Antarctica threaten to escape; The *Purple Sapphire,* superscience, lost races in Central Tibet, survivors of the Great Race. 4 illustrations by Frank R. Paul. v + 532pp.
21180-0 Paperbound $3.00

SEVEN SCIENCE FICTION NOVELS, H. G. Wells. The standard collection of the great novels. Complete, unabridged. *First Men in the Moon, Island of Dr. Moreau, War of the Worlds, Food of the Gods, Invisible Man, Time Machine, In the Days of the Comet.* Not only science fiction fans, but every educated person owes it to himself to read these novels. 1015pp.
20264-X Clothbound $5.00

LAST AND FIRST MEN AND STAR MAKER, TWO SCIENCE FICTION NOVELS, Olaf Stapledon. Greatest future histories in science fiction. In the first, human intelligence is the "hero," through strange paths of evolution, interplanetary invasions, incredible technologies, near extinctions and reemergences. Star Maker describes the quest of a band of star rovers for intelligence itself, through time and space: weird inhuman civilizations, crustacean minds, symbiotic worlds, etc. Complete, unabridged. v + 438pp.   21962-3 Paperbound $2.50

THREE PROPHETIC NOVELS, H. G. WELLS. Stages of a consistently planned future for mankind. *When the Sleeper Wakes,* and *A Story of the Days to Come,* anticipate *Brave New World* and *1984,* in the 21st Century; *The Time Machine,* only complete version in print, shows farther future and the end of mankind. All show Wells's greatest gifts as storyteller and novelist. Edited by E. F. Bleiler. x + 335pp.   (USO) 20605-X Paperbound $2.25

THE DEVIL'S DICTIONARY, Ambrose Bierce. America's own Oscar Wilde—Ambrose Bierce—offers his barbed iconoclastic wisdom in over 1,000 definitions hailed by H. L. Mencken as "some of the most gorgeous witticisms in the English language." 145pp.   20487-1 Paperbound $1.25

MAX AND MORITZ, Wilhelm Busch. Great children's classic, father of comic strip, of two bad boys, Max and Moritz. Also Ker and Plunk (Plisch und Plumm), Cat and Mouse, Deceitful Henry, Ice-Peter, The Boy and the Pipe, and five other pieces. Original German, with English translation. Edited by H. Arthur Klein; translations by various hands and H. Arthur Klein. vi + 216pp.
                          20181-3 Paperbound $2.00

PIGS IS PIGS AND OTHER FAVORITES, Ellis Parker Butler. The title story is one of the best humor short stories, as Mike Flannery obfuscates biology and English. Also included, That Pup of Murchison's, The Great American Pie Company, and Perkins of Portland. 14 illustrations. v + 109pp.   21532-6 Paperbound $1.00

THE PETERKIN PAPERS, Lucretia P. Hale. It takes genius to be as stupidly mad as the Peterkins, as they decide to become wise, celebrate the "Fourth," keep a cow, and otherwise strain the resources of the Lady from Philadelphia. Basic book of American humor. 153 illustrations. 219pp.   20794-3 Paperbound $1.50

PERRAULT'S FAIRY TALES, translated by A. E. Johnson and S. R. Littlewood, with 34 full-page illustrations by Gustave Doré. All the original Perrault stories—Cinderella, Sleeping Beauty, Bluebeard, Little Red Riding Hood, Puss in Boots, Tom Thumb, etc.—with their witty verse morals and the magnificent illustrations of Doré. One of the five or six great books of European fairy tales. viii + 117pp. 8⅛ x 11.   22311-6 Paperbound $2.00

OLD HUNGARIAN FAIRY TALES, Baroness Orczy. Favorites translated and adapted by author of the *Scarlet Pimpernel.* Eight fairy tales include "The Suitors of Princess Fire-Fly," "The Twin Hunchbacks," "Mr. Cuttlefish's Love Story," and "The Enchanted Cat." This little volume of magic and adventure will captivate children as it has for generations. 90 drawings by Montagu Barstow. 96pp.
                          (USO) 22293-4 Paperbound $1.95

THE RED FAIRY BOOK, Andrew Lang. Lang's color fairy books have long been children's favorites. This volume includes Rapunzel, Jack and the Bean-stalk and 35 other stories, familiar and unfamiliar. 4 plates, 93 illustrations x + 367pp.
21673-X Paperbound $2.50

THE BLUE FAIRY BOOK, Andrew Lang. Lang's tales come from all countries and all times. Here are 37 tales from Grimm, the Arabian Nights, Greek Mythology, and other fascinating sources. 8 plates, 130 illustrations. xi + 390pp.
21437-0 Paperbound $2.50

HOUSEHOLD STORIES BY THE BROTHERS GRIMM. Classic English-language edition of the well-known tales — Rumpelstiltskin, Snow White, Hansel and Gretel, The Twelve Brothers, Faithful John, Rapunzel, Tom Thumb (52 stories in all). Translated into simple, straightforward English by Lucy Crane. Ornamented with head-pieces, vignettes, elaborate decorative initials and a dozen full-page illustrations by Walter Crane. x + 269pp.
21080-4 Paperbound $2.50

THE MERRY ADVENTURES OF ROBIN HOOD, Howard Pyle. The finest modern versions of the traditional ballads and tales about the great English outlaw. Howard Pyle's complete prose version, with every word, every illustration of the first edition. Do not confuse this facsimile of the original (1883) with modern editions that change text or illustrations. 23 plates plus many page decorations. xxii + 296pp.
22043-5 Paperbound $2.50

THE STORY OF KING ARTHUR AND HIS KNIGHTS, Howard Pyle. The finest children's version of the life of King Arthur; brilliantly retold by Pyle, with 48 of his most imaginative illustrations. xviii + 313pp. 6⅛ x 9¼.
21445-1 Paperbound $2.50

THE WONDERFUL WIZARD OF OZ, L. Frank Baum. America's finest children's book in facsimile of first edition with all Denslow illustrations in full color. The edition a child should have. Introduction by Martin Gardner. 23 color plates, scores of drawings. iv + 267pp.
20691-2 Paperbound $2.25

THE MARVELOUS LAND OF OZ, L. Frank Baum. The second Oz book, every bit as imaginative as the Wizard. The hero is a boy named Tip, but the Scarecrow and the Tin Woodman are back, as is the Oz magic. 16 color plates, 120 drawings by John R. Neill. 287pp.
20692-0 Paperbound $2.50

THE MAGICAL MONARCH OF MO, L. Frank Baum. Remarkable adventures in a land even stranger than Oz. The best of Baum's books not in the Oz series. 15 color plates and dozens of drawings by Frank Verbeck. xviii + 237pp.
21892-9 Paperbound $2.00

THE BAD CHILD'S BOOK OF BEASTS, MORE BEASTS FOR WORSE CHILDREN, A MORAL ALPHABET, Hilaire Belloc. Three complete humor classics in one volume. Be kind to the frog, and do not call him names . . . and 28 other whimsical animals. Familiar favorites and some not so well known. Illustrated by Basil Blackwell. 156pp.
(USO) 20749-8 Paperbound $1.25

EAST O' THE SUN AND WEST O' THE MOON, George W. Dasent. Considered the best of all translations of these Norwegian folk tales, this collection has been enjoyed by generations of children (and folklorists too). Includes True and Untrue, Why the Sea is Salt, East O' the Sun and West O' the Moon, Why the Bear is Stumpy-Tailed, Boots and the Troll, The Cock and the Hen, Rich Peter the Pedlar, and 52 more. The only edition with all 59 tales. 77 illustrations by Erik Werenskiold and Theodor Kittelsen. xv + 418pp.   22521-6 Paperbound $3.00

GOOPS AND HOW TO BE THEM, Gelett Burgess. Classic of tongue-in-cheek humor, masquerading as etiquette book. 87 verses, twice as many cartoons, show mischievous Goops as they demonstrate to children virtues of table manners, neatness, courtesy, etc. Favorite for generations. viii + 88pp. 6½ x 9¼.
22233-0 Paperbound $1.25

ALICE'S ADVENTURES UNDER GROUND, Lewis Carroll. The first version, quite different from the final *Alice in Wonderland,* printed out by Carroll himself with his own illustrations. Complete facsimile of the "million dollar" manuscript Carroll gave to Alice Liddell in 1864. Introduction by Martin Gardner. viii + 96pp. Title and dedication pages in color.   21482-6 Paperbound $1.25

THE BROWNIES, THEIR BOOK, Palmer Cox. Small as mice, cunning as foxes, exuberant and full of mischief, the Brownies go to the zoo, toy shop, seashore, circus, etc., in 24 verse adventures and 266 illustrations. Long a favorite, since their first appearance in St. Nicholas Magazine. xi + 144pp. 6⅝ x 9¼.
21265-3 Paperbound $1.75

SONGS OF CHILDHOOD, Walter De La Mare. Published (under the pseudonym Walter Ramal) when De La Mare was only 29, this charming collection has long been a favorite children's book. A facsimile of the first edition in paper, the 47 poems capture the simplicity of the nursery rhyme and the ballad, including such lyrics as I Met Eve, Tartary, The Silver Penny. vii + 106pp. 21972-0 Paperbound $1.25

THE COMPLETE NONSENSE OF EDWARD LEAR, Edward Lear. The finest 19th-century humorist-cartoonist in full: all nonsense limericks, zany alphabets, Owl and Pussycat, songs, nonsense botany, and more than 500 illustrations by Lear himself. Edited by Holbrook Jackson. xxix + 287pp.   (USO) 20167-8 Paperbound $2.00

BILLY WHISKERS: THE AUTOBIOGRAPHY OF A GOAT, Frances Trego Montgomery. A favorite of children since the early 20th century, here are the escapades of that rambunctious, irresistible and mischievous goat—Billy Whiskers. Much in the spirit of *Peck's Bad Boy,* this is a book that children never tire of reading or hearing. All the original familiar illustrations by W. H. Fry are included: 6 color plates, 18 black and white drawings. 159pp.   22345-0 Paperbound $2.00

MOTHER GOOSE MELODIES. Faithful republication of the fabulously rare Munroe and Francis "copyright 1833" Boston edition—the most important Mother Goose collection, usually referred to as the "original." Familiar rhymes plus many rare ones, with wonderful old woodcut illustrations. Edited by E. F. Bleiler. 128pp. 4½ x 6⅜.   22577-1 Paperbound $1.25

TWO LITTLE SAVAGES; BEING THE ADVENTURES OF TWO BOYS WHO LIVED AS INDIANS AND WHAT THEY LEARNED, Ernest Thompson Seton. Great classic of nature and boyhood provides a vast range of woodlore in most palatable form, a genuinely entertaining story. Two farm boys build a teepee in woods and live in it for a month, working out Indian solutions to living problems, star lore, birds and animals, plants, etc. 293 illustrations. vii + 286pp.

20985-7 Paperbound $2.50

PETER PIPER'S PRACTICAL PRINCIPLES OF PLAIN & PERFECT PRONUNCIATION. Alliterative jingles and tongue-twisters of surprising charm, that made their first appearance in America about 1830. Republished in full with the spirited woodcut illustrations from this earliest American edition. 32pp. 4½ x 6⅜.

22560-7 Paperbound $1.00

SCIENCE EXPERIMENTS AND AMUSEMENTS FOR CHILDREN, Charles Vivian. 73 easy experiments, requiring only materials found at home or easily available, such as candles, coins, steel wool, etc.; illustrate basic phenomena like vacuum, simple chemical reaction, etc. All safe. Modern, well-planned. Formerly *Science Games for Children.* 102 photos, numerous drawings. 96pp. 6⅛ x 9¼.

21856-2 Paperbound $1.25

AN INTRODUCTION TO CHESS MOVES AND TACTICS SIMPLY EXPLAINED, Leonard Barden. Informal intermediate introduction, quite strong in explaining reasons for moves. Covers basic material, tactics, important openings, traps, positional play in middle game, end game. Attempts to isolate patterns and recurrent configurations. Formerly *Chess.* 58 figures. 102pp. (USO) 21210-6 Paperbound $1.25

LASKER'S MANUAL OF CHESS, Dr. Emanuel Lasker. Lasker was not only one of the five great World Champions, he was also one of the ablest expositors, theorists, and analysts. In many ways, his Manual, permeated with his philosophy of battle, filled with keen insights, is one of the greatest works ever written on chess. Filled with analyzed games by the great players. A single-volume library that will profit almost any chess player, beginner or master. 308 diagrams. xli x 349pp.

20640-8 Paperbound $2.75

THE MASTER BOOK OF MATHEMATICAL RECREATIONS, Fred Schuh. In opinion of many the finest work ever prepared on mathematical puzzles, stunts, recreations; exhaustively thorough explanations of mathematics involved, analysis of effects, citation of puzzles and games. Mathematics involved is elementary. Translated by F. Göbel. 194 figures. xxiv + 430pp.

22134-2 Paperbound $3.00

MATHEMATICS, MAGIC AND MYSTERY, Martin Gardner. Puzzle editor for Scientific American explains mathematics behind various mystifying tricks: card tricks, stage "mind reading," coin and match tricks, counting out games, geometric dissections, etc. Probability sets, theory of numbers clearly explained. Also provides more than 400 tricks, guaranteed to work, that you can do. 135 illustrations. xii + 176pp.

20338-2 Paperbound $1.50

MATHEMATICAL PUZZLES FOR BEGINNERS AND ENTHUSIASTS, Geoffrey Mott-Smith. 189 puzzles from easy to difficult—involving arithmetic, logic, algebra, properties of digits, probability, etc.—for enjoyment and mental stimulus. Explanation of mathematical principles behind the puzzles. 135 illustrations. viii + 248pp.

20198-8 Paperbound $1.75

PAPER FOLDING FOR BEGINNERS, William D. Murray and Francis J. Rigney. Easiest book on the market, clearest instructions on making interesting, beautiful origami. Sail boats, cups, roosters, frogs that move legs, bonbon boxes, standing birds, etc. 40 projects; more than 275 diagrams and photographs. 94pp.

20713-7 Paperbound $1.00

TRICKS AND GAMES ON THE POOL TABLE, Fred Herrmann. 79 tricks and games— some solitaires, some for two or more players, some competitive games—to entertain you between formal games. Mystifying shots and throws, unusual caroms, tricks involving such props as cork, coins, a hat, etc. Formerly *Fun on the Pool Table*. 77 figures. 95pp.

21814-7 Paperbound $1.00

HAND SHADOWS TO BE THROWN UPON THE WALL: A SERIES OF NOVEL AND AMUSING FIGURES FORMED BY THE HAND, Henry Bursill. Delightful picturebook from great-grandfather's day shows how to make 18 different hand shadows: a bird that flies, duck that quacks, dog that wags his tail, camel, goose, deer, boy, turtle, etc. Only book of its sort. vi + 33pp. 6½ x 9¼. 21779-5 Paperbound $1.00

WHITTLING AND WOODCARVING, E. J. Tangerman. 18th printing of best book on market. "If you can cut a potato you can carve" toys and puzzles, chains, chessmen, caricatures, masks, frames, woodcut blocks, surface patterns, much more. Information on tools, woods, techniques. Also goes into serious wood sculpture from Middle Ages to present, East and West. 464 photos, figures. x + 293pp.

20965-2 Paperbound $2.00

HISTORY OF PHILOSOPHY, Julián Marias. Possibly the clearest, most easily followed, best planned, most useful one-volume history of philosophy on the market; neither skimpy nor overfull. Full details on system of every major philosopher and dozens of less important thinkers from pre-Socratics up to Existentialism and later. Strong on many European figures usually omitted. Has gone through dozens of editions in Europe. 1966 edition, translated by Stanley Appelbaum and Clarence Strowbridge. xviii + 505pp.

21739-6 Paperbound $3.00

YOGA: A SCIENTIFIC EVALUATION, Kovoor T. Behanan. Scientific but non-technical study of physiological results of yoga exercises; done under auspices of Yale U. Relations to Indian thought, to psychoanalysis, etc. 16 photos. xxiii + 270pp.

20505-3 Paperbound $2.50

Prices subject to change without notice.
Available at your book dealer or write for free catalogue to Dept. GI, Dover Publications, Inc., 180 Varick St., N. Y., N. Y. 10014. Dover publishes more than 150 books each year on science, elementary and advanced mathematics, biology, music, art, literary history, social sciences and other areas.